Leadership for Quality and Accountability in Education

What is the role of leadership in developing strategies that enhance learning outcomes?

Leadership for Quality and Accountability in Education addresses the interconnected issues of quality and accountability in the education system and provides a coherent framework within which these issues can be analysed. The authors outline the significance of promoting quality in all educational establishments and go on to discuss: why quality and accountability have become so essential to the framework of leadership in education; and how quality and accountability have been utilised on a national and international scale and what the defining characteristics of these terms are.

The book is divided into three sections which explore three linked key aspects:

- Part I focuses on the concept and nature of quality and accountability and the process of developing a culture of quality.
- Part II addresses the issues of managing staff and resources, leadership for high-quality teaching and learning, and relationships with stakeholders.
- Part III considers the impact and prospect of quality and accountability, including internal evaluation and external inspection.

The book will appeal to educational leaders and managers, advisors and inspectors, and academic researchers. It will also be of particular relevance to Masters and doctoral degree students specialising in school leadership and management.

Mark Brundrett is Professor of Educational Research in the Faculty of Education, Community and Leisure at Liverpool John Moores University, UK.

Christopher Rhodes is Senior Lecturer in Educational Leadership in the School of Education at the University of Birmingham, UK.

D0145281

Leadership for learning series
Series editors: Clive Dimmock, Mark Brundrett and Les Bell

The study of educational leadership makes little sense unless it is in relation to who the leaders are, how they are leading, what is being led, and with what effect. Based on the premise that learning is at the heart of leadership and that leaders themselves should be learners, the Leadership for Learning series explores the connections between educational leadership, policy, curriculum, human resources and accountability. Each book in the series approaches its subject matter through a three-fold structure of process, themes and impact.

Other titles in the series:

Education Policy
Les Bell and Howard Stevenson

Leading Learning
Tom O'Donoghue and Simon Clarke

Human Resource Management in Education
Justine Mercer, Bernard Barker and Richard Bird

Forthcoming:

Leadership in Education
Clive Dimmock

Leadership for Quality and Accountability in Education

Mark Brundrett and
Christopher Rhodes

Routledge
Taylor & Francis Group

LONDON AND NEW YORK

First published 2011
by Routledge
2 Park Square, Milton Park, Abingdon, Oxon, OX14 4RN

Simultaneously published in the USA and Canada
by Routledge
270 Madison Avenue, New York, NY 10016

Routledge is an imprint of the Taylor & Francis Group, an informa business

Typeset in Garamond by Swales & Willis Ltd, Exeter, Devon
Printed and bound in Great Britain by CPI Antony Rowe, Chippenham, Wiltshire

British Library Cataloguing in Publication Data
A catalogue record for this book is available from the British Library

Library of Congress Cataloging-in-Publication Data
A catalog record has been requested for this book

ISBN13: 978–0–415–37873–4 (hbk)
ISBN13: 978–0–415–37874–1 (pbk)
ISBN13: 978–0–203–85293–4 (ebk)

Contents

Notes on authors

Mark Brundrett worked in secondary, middle and primary schools and was a head-teacher for several years prior to entering higher education. He has subsequently worked in a number of university departments as Lecturer, Senior Lecturer and Professor of Education. He is currently Professor of Educational Research in the Faculty of Education, Community and Leisure at Liverpool John Moores University, UK.

Christopher Rhodes worked in schools and colleges for 14 years prior to taking up a post in higher education. He was previously the Director of Postgraduate Studies in the School of Education at the University of Wolverhampton and currently holds the post of Senior Lecturer in Educational Leadership in the School of Education at the University of Birmingham, UK.

Introduction

The journey from autonomy to quality and accountability in education

The period since the 1980s could quite justifiably be called the era of quality and accountability in education. Schools, colleges and universities, both in the UK and internationally, have experienced a period of unprecedented government intervention in terms of the curriculum that is taught and the ways in which educational establishments are monitored. Whilst the terms 'quality' and 'accountability' would have been familiar to those working in education a generation ago, their relevance to the daily life of work would have been very considerably less than they are today. For many, if not all, of those working as teachers or lecturers prior to the latter years of the twentieth century the central notion that governed their working lives would have been that of the autonomous professional. Once they had received their degree, diploma, or professional certification and some appropriate experience they had a right to consider that they should make decisions about what went on in their classroom or lecture theatre without undue interference from superiors or external agency unless there was some very clear reason for intervention.

This did not mean that there was a lack of concern for quality, nor did it mean that accountability systems did not exist. Indeed, there was a general societal expectation that professional educators would take pride in their work, in the way that they related to pupils and students and in the outcomes that those in their care achieved in examinations. Equally, in almost all countries there were both local and national systems of external inspection. For instance in England, Local Authority advisers had a responsibility to monitor the quality of education in the schools under their supervision and a national system of inspection existed in the form of the highly respected national inspection agency that had operated since early in the reign of Queen Victoria under the title of Her Majesty's Inspectors (HMI). However, the remit of Local Authority officers tasked with monitoring school quality was often unclear with little, if any, disjunction between the role of inspector and that of adviser; neither was there a generally agreed model of local inspection. HMI did operate to a clear and agreed methodology but the incidence of their inspections was comparatively infrequent and some teachers might never be subject to such an inspection in their whole career should they have the fortune to move from one school to another with sufficient regularity. By contrast, the modern system of inspection of quality operated by the Office for Standards in Education (Ofsted) is comparatively frequent and there is relatively little uncertainty about their role. Until the late twentieth century universities in England cherished their independence based on a charter of foundation that each received from the Sovereign. Although some of this independence remains, these universities have now been joined by 'new universities', composed of former polytechnics and colleges, which brought with them experience of more bureaucratic quality regimes. All English universities are now subject to forms of quality audit both for the subjects they teach, by the Quality Assurance Agency (QAA), and for the research they carry out, by a system which was originally known as the Research Assessment Exercise (RAE), restyled the Research Excellence Framework (REF) in 2009. England is by no means alone in this revolution in quality systems in education and similar developments have occurred in many countries around the globe.

The changes in the understanding of the terms quality and accountability over recent years are not, however, confined to a metaphorical re-arrangement of the furniture of inspection regimes in terms of changes to the titles and the remit of agencies. In fact there has been a revolution in the meaning and significance of the terms quality and accountability. As will be discussed in detail later in this text, this is in part because of the importation of business-orientated approaches to quality into educational institutions, part of a general reappraisal of the role of the state that has occurred in many nations. The journey to these new conceptions of quality has been complex and difficult and is made all the more contentious by the fact that there are those who would argue, with some justification, that we now live in an era of performativity, a concept that will be explored in more detail in Chapter 1, whereby education has become subsumed by the state. However, when perceived in the best of lights, the quality and accountability movement has been about ensuring that educational institutions have even greater concern for excellence in what they do.

The rest of this introductory chapter commences the exploration of the journey towards new conceptions of quality and accountability, explores the origins of the modern concept of quality and the rise of quality and accountability systems in education, then sets out the focus and structure of this text.

The development of the concept of quality

In setting out on a text which is designed to address the linked topics of quality and accountability in education it is important to consider the origins of the modern quality movement. The antecedents of contemporary notions of quality can be seen in nineteenth century industrial processes where a concern for standardization, conformity and mass production became the norm. Such attitudes can be seen to spread from Britain into Germany, France and much of western Europe, but found their ultimate expression in the 'Fordism' of the early twentieth century in the United States of America (US). The origins of the term 'accountability' are similarly arcane but can be divined from the root word 'account' and the requirement for a detailed record of financial expenditure that became necessary with the development of banking houses in the eighteenth century. However, for those working in educational institutions it may come as a surprise that many of the modern conceptions of quality emerged in the context of Japanese industrial regeneration after the Second World War. The movement was inspired and developed by two Americans, Deming and Juran, whose early work was concerned with methods of measuring quality in the engineering industry. The success of Japanese industry in the 1960s and 1970s was largely credited to the quality movement and it is interesting to conjecture whether the comparative decline in competitiveness in Japanese industry since the late 1980s has influenced subsequent thinking on quality.

The work of Deming was adopted comparatively slowly in the West, largely because he wrote few texts or articles, preferring instead to work directly with industry or hold seminars to discuss his work. Nonetheless, Deming's writing has been highly influential (see Deming, 1982) and his work has inspired individuals, companies and social organizations such as schools and colleges to reconsider the way they operate to enhance quality. In relation to the more recent developments in accountability in education explored in the latter chapters of this text, it is crucial to note that for Deming, the concept of inspection was irrelevant; he saw it as an add-on that is often ineffective and costly and should be unnecessary, since quality should be paramount throughout the system. Whilst Deming has been criticized for the comparative simplicity of some of his theories Juran, in contrast, has been recognized as the most intellectually profound of the management theorists and it was Juran who famously defined quality as 'fitness for purpose' (Juran, 1989).

The key concepts of Deming and Juran were extended and re-interpreted by Crosby, who remains one of the most significant and influential writers in the United States of America and Europe (see, for instance, Crosby, 1979). However, it was perhaps Peters' and Waterman's text, *In Search of Excellence* (Peters and Waterman, 1982), which reinforced the fundamental message that customer satisfaction is paramount, and which gained a wider audience for notions of quality and their applicability to other contexts such as education. Nonetheless, it was not until the late 1980s that there was a major awakening of interest in the education sector, first of all in Local Education Authorities (LEAs) and tertiary education, and then in schools. The importation of quality models from the wider management sector rapidly increased in pace in the 1990s and early 2000s and eventually influenced the development of national standards and the inspection regimes that would become operant in all phases of education (West-Burnham, 1992).

The importance of this historical context lies in the fact that both quality and accountability have suffered from a difficult relationship with the education sector. The reasons can be seen in both the locus and the key concepts associated with the rise of quality systems. As already noted, there are many in education who deplore the importation of what are, in essence, business models into the social context of education. It is easy to see why ideas that find their origins in the mass production of industrial items are sometimes considered to be anathema to those concerned with the development of young minds. On the other hand there are those who consider that the use of quality and accountability models are essential in an era of local financial management of educational institutions, when leaders of schools, colleges and universities are required to manage very large budgets and 'plant and equipment' that may be worth many millions of pounds. These tensions should be kept in mind throughout the reading of this text and the problematic nature of quality and accountability in education will be explored in greater detail in Chapter 1.

The rise of quality and accountability systems in education

As noted above, for much of the twentieth century the work of pioneers in quality such as Deming and Juran had little impact on educational institutions. Schools, colleges and higher education establishments were considered accountable to local stakeholders such as parents, governors, local government or, in the case of many universities, to a self-regulating body such as a senate. Somewhat ironically, however, the increasingly global phenomenon of local or devolved management of educational institutions, allied to an enhanced focus on standards-based education, has led to a massively increased interest in the interconnected issues of quality and accountability. 'Hard edged' systems of quality and external inspection are increasingly being replaced by 'hybrid systems' that attempt to ensure ownership of quality systems at practitioner, institutional and systemic levels. This text is designed to scrutinize such trends and attempts to subject the challenges, dangers and opportunities inherent in these developments to detailed scrutiny.

This is not a straightforward task, as understandings of quality are relative and are very likely to vary depending on whether you are, for example, a learner, a parent, a staff member or a quality auditor. A study of quality and accountability raises questions concerning what we are seeking to probe the quality of, for whom, and why, as well as what we are seeking to offer an account of, to whom, and why we are offering such an account. There is general agreement that the central purposes of education show commonality across all sectors of education and hold high the importance of the quality of the learning experience and subsequent learner outcomes. However, whilst few would argue against the notion that educational organizations wish to serve the needs of their stakeholders to best effect, the questions of what structures and cultures best support quality improvement, are feasible, acceptable and sustainable within educational organizations are more problematic and open to debate. Equally, one might ask how such structures and cultures should be chosen and developed and whether it is best that they should employ internal or external quality frameworks. To be accountable to the many stakeholders in education entails offering an account of performance and to justify this in relation to established or expected standards. It is right that educational organizations and their leaders should account in these terms for their organization's performance both internally and externally, especially in view of the large amounts of public money invested. Whether the rise of decentralization and market accountability in education has served the associated purpose of improvement, however, remains an ongoing subject of debate. As educational organizations spend time and effort gathering and analysing data to understand where they are now and how they might do better, the question of balance between improvement and the effort involved in accountability is raised. Achieving service for those seeking accountability and those seeking improvement offers challenges for leaders, managers and their staff in schools, colleges and in higher education. In these permeable organizations leaders will need to inspire, enable commitment and engage measures to monitor and evaluate all that they do. This is a complex area of education and one which this book will attempt to explore.

The focus of this text

The key focus of this text is on the role of leadership and its direct relationship with quality and accountability in enhancing learning outcomes. It is the belief of the authors that texts on quality in education have tended to take one of three forms: the development of broad analytical models through which the quality process can be informed; critiques, often negative in nature, of the notion of quality and associated systems of external accountability; or practical guides to enhancing quality or achieving positive outcomes in external review. These relatively fragmented approaches often fail to provide a cogent account of the quality process within a clearly articulated framework for analysis. It is often difficult for those working in schools that are subject to quality systems and allied inspection regimes to make sense of the underlying assumptions on which such systems are based. Equally, those working as academic commentators or policy implementers may be unaware of the impact of quality systems upon the day-to-day activities of schools and other educational organizations. The main purpose of this book, therefore, is to provide a coherent framework within which notions of quality and accountability can be analysed and subjected to rigorous scrutiny whilst retaining a clear picture of the impact of the quality process in institutions. The authors have drawn on research evidence and the most recent quality frameworks that operate in educational contexts. From the outset it was intended that as well as being 'academic' and relating to research, the text would intertwine key issues for professional practice in the form of suggested readings, activities and key reflection points. The text is thus designed to have broad appeal to practitioners across all phases of the education system; educational leaders and managers, advisers and inspectors, and academic researchers.

The structure and content of this text

The text is divided into three parts, addressing process, themes, and impact in quality and accountability in education. Thus, to elaborate further, the text addresses the following:

- In Part I consideration is given to the nature and processes of quality and accountability in an era of performativity, both generally and more specifically in the field of education, through a detailed examination of the development of quality regimes and the concepts associated with them. Process is addressed in two ways: first, in terms of the process whereby notions of quality and accountability have been developed and defined and second, in terms of the process through which a culture of quality can be developed.
- In Part II key themes in quality and accountability and their implications are explored. These include the consequences of creating a culture of quality for

resource management, enhancing teaching and learning, and relationships with stakeholders.

- In Part III the impact and prospect of quality and accountability are examined in terms of the major effects on education of the comparatively recent intrusion of quality frameworks into educational institutions. This analysis is provided especially in relation to new and emergent frameworks of quality that are increasingly setting the agenda for the ways in which schools and further and higher education institutions are managed and led.

In Chapter 1 we note that quality has come to the forefront of educational thinking in a period when central government has intervened in all aspects of social welfare. Debate continues about which models of quality are most appropriate to education – business models or those driven by notions of social capital and inherent worthiness. The opening chapter thus seeks to unpack the conceptual confusion that surrounds these issues and argues that new models are required that ensure rigour in curriculum delivery and learning outcomes whilst protecting professional autonomy. In Chapter 2 we ask the question 'quality for whom?' and examine the overlapping and sometimes competing conceptions of quality as they relate to the three levels of learner–practitioner relationships; school-wide quality; and system-wide quality. Chapter 3 examines the process of developing a culture of quality and posits that if educational organizations are to enhance quality in all aspects of their work they must explore and exemplify key features of quality in all aspects of their work. It also examines how and whether cultures in educational organizations can be developed that build in quality enhancement systems from 'the ground up'.

In Chapter 4 we focus on managing staff and resources for quality education and argue that lessons from research into institutional effectiveness and improvement reveal that the deployment and management of staff and resources is one of the keys to enhancing quality. In this exploration we address such vital contemporary issues as recruitment, retention and development of staff and we will examine recent innovations such as performance-related pay and its possible influence on quality. In Chapter 5 we note that recent developments in the field of educational leadership and management have re-emphasized that leadership must focus on educational outcomes and that leadership for learning is central to enhancing the quality of schooling. This chapter explores the relationship between leadership at all levels, in schools and other educational organizations, in order to enhance the quality of teaching and learning experienced by pupils and students. Chapter 6 draws on the notion that schools are 'permeable organizations' that have myriad, and sometimes competing, sets of stakeholder requirements that must be addressed. This chapter will explore the nature of accountability in educational organizations. Chapter 7 considers the complex sets of relationships that educational leaders must manage if their institutions are to be successful, including those with parents, students, and local and national government authorities.

Chapters 8 and 9 seek to outline two alternative, but not mutually exclusive, models of quality enhancement. In the first of these chapters we focus on self-evaluation and the internal structures, attitudes and attributes that can enhance quality. Chapter 9 goes on to examine key issues in the external inspection of educational organizations, including recent developments in the inspection frameworks. Finally, in Chapter 10, we attempt to go beyond quality and accountability by returning to some of the themes introduced right at the start of the text in order to investigate the ways in which educational organizations might attempt to go beyond some of the more reductivist elements of the quality regimes that have held sway in education in recent years.

For most of this text the discussion is cross-phase and cross-sector. However, although the increased focus on quality is ubiquitous and much of the nature of the discussion is very similar in all phases of education, some of the discourse is nuanced and the specific approaches taken can vary. For this reason the main focus is on schools, since they remain numerically the largest and chronologically the longest sector in education and, where deemed appropriate and helpful to the reader, separate sections have been included that deal with the specifics of further and higher education policy and practice.

A note on the positional commitment of the text

We have outlined that the twin concepts of quality and accountability are contentious when applied to education. The writers have attempted to take a balanced view of the topic and throughout the text we attempt to outline the nature of quality and accountability and the purported benefits of the implementation of a culture of quality in terms of enhancing teaching and learning. At the same time we have endeavoured to respect the associated critique that has developed in depth over recent years. This has been a difficult balance to find but our aim has been to inform, to analyse and to challenge throughout.

Whatever the viewpoint or sector of the reader, we hope that this text will be of help in prompting further thinking about their own practice and research agenda and that it will encourage further exploration of this large, important and complex field.

Part I

The nature and process of quality and accountability

1 The concept of quality

Introduction

'Quality' has come to the forefront of educational thinking in a period when central governments in many nations, including the United Kingdom (UK), have intervened increasingly in all aspects of social welfare. It is a concomitant of this intervention that debate continues about which models of quality are most appropriate to state-funded organizations such as schools, colleges and universities – business models or those driven by notions of social capital and inherent worthiness. As the power of the state has been extended, so a new form of 'contract' has emerged between government and educational institutions. In essence this contract consists of the notion that central government will devolve power, including financial control, outwards whilst at the same time increasing the regulatory framework within which institutions operate. It is an inevitable element of this revised framework of governance that institutions are increasingly required to account for the quality of their work and the outputs that they produce. Not surprisingly these changes have not been without difficulty and those tasked with the delivery of services have found the transition problematic. Not least of these problems is exactly what we mean by terms such as 'quality'. For this reason the opening chapter of this text will unpack the conceptual turmoil which surrounds quality in education and so this chapter will examine the problematic nature of quality and some modern conceptions associated with the topic. More specifically, it will explore:

- performativity and education;
- the 'problem' with quality;
- concepts associated with quality such as quality control versus quality assurance;
- Total Quality Management in education;
- the challenges associated with the application of business models of quality to the context of education.

We conclude by emphasizing that although there are those who continue to argue that quality models should have nothing to do with the social setting of educational organizations, we cannot ignore the fact that quality systems have become an integral part of educational systems across the world and the language of quality has become commonplace in educational settings.

Performativity and education

For some in education the new 'contract' between state and educational professionals, described earlier, has been imposed by central governments and has brought in an era of 'performativity' which is largely unwelcome. The concept of performativity is complex and stretches across a variety of fields in the social sciences including linguistics, gender studies and sociology. Lyotard (1984: 46) suggests that the defining feature of performativity is that it involves the subsumption of education to the efficient functioning of the social system. According to this model, education is no longer to be concerned with the pursuit of ideals such as personal autonomy or emancipation, but with the means, techniques or skills that contribute to the efficient operation of the state in the world market (Marshall, 2004). As Ball notes, performativity is a technology, a culture and a mode of regulation, or even a system of 'terror', that employs judgement as a means of control and change (Ball, 2001: 143). Within this system the performance of individuals or entire organizations serves as a measure of productivity, displays of quality or moments of inspection. These encapsulate the worth or quality of such individuals and organizations within a 'field of judgement' (Ball, 2001: 143) and 'accountability' and 'competition' are the lingua franca of this 'discourse of power' (Lyotard, 1984: 46).

For our purposes we might define an era of performativity in education as one in which the notion of the autonomous professional has become redundant and has been replaced by a state-imposed regime based on the external measurement of quality through an onerous and burdensome system of inspection and testing. For those who subscribe to this model it is easy to see why notions of quality and accountability, when applied to education, are seen as undesirable. This is a powerful and persuasive analysis that has become highly influential in recent years and it will form something of background or *leitmotif* to Chapters 1–3 of the text. However, even if one does not accept this increasingly dominant portrayal of central intervention, quality remains a difficult notion when applied to education because of the slippery nature of the term and it is to this that we now turn.

The problem of defining what we mean by 'quality' in education

Despite the fact that business models of leadership and management only became ubiquitous in education some time after they had influenced international companies, much of the public debate on education in recent years has centred on issues of quality in ways that would be familiar to many in private industry. In the broadest sense, whether in industry or in education, quality enhancement relates to achieving better outcomes and dictates that improving quality is inevitably one of the most important tasks facing any organization, whether it be educational or otherwise. However, despite its importance, many people involved in education find quality an enigmatic concept because one person's idea of quality often conflicts with another's (Sallis, 2002: 1). This is because definitions of desired outcomes for schools may vary widely, from those who wish to ensure that schools produce citizens who are happy, healthy and socially well adjusted to those whose overriding focus is to produce the best-qualified learners in terms of academic achievement.

Some attempts made to define quality illustrate the 'elusive' (Green, 1994: 12), 'slippery' (Walsh, 1994: 52), 'problematic' (Liston, 1999: 4) and 'controversial' (CHES, 1994: 18) nature of the concept. Crosby (1979: 9) defines quality as: 'the Zero Defects concept . . . the thought that everyone should do things right the first time'. On the other hand there is an alternative conception of quality which is primarily focused on continuous improvement and rejects 'getting it right the first time' or 'zero defects'. According to this theory mistakes are to be expected and, in some senses, embraced because they represent a source of a new learning experience and of progress (see, for instance, Nightingale and O'Neil, 1994: 165). Juran (1989: 15) suggested that 'quality is fitness for use' but such an approach is especially flawed in relation to education. For instance, in response to this conception, Green (1994: 15) stated that 'the problem with this definition of quality . . . is that it is difficult to be clear what the purposes of higher education should be'. An additional weakness of the 'fit-ness for purpose' definition is that it also omits the notion that some institutions may be 'better' in some way than others, in the sense that the purposes they serve may be more comprehensive or more desirable than those of their competitors (Goodlad, 1995: 8).

A synthesis of the various approaches to defining quality needs to acknowledge that there are a great many competing views of the nature of the concept. Whilst some see quality as implicit and indefinable others take what might be termed a measurement view of quality, which relates to satisfactory conformance to some pre-defined standard. The apparently competing and overlapping views can make it diffi-cult to make sense of a topic which appears, superficially, to be transparent but is complex and challenging when examined in detail (Murgatroyd and Morgan, 1993: 45–46).

Sallis (2002: 23) points out that 'fitness for purpose' or use of terminology implying 'measuring up to specification' is a 'producer definition of quality'. He writes that quality can also be defined as: 'that which best satisfies and exceeds customer needs and wants'. This is sometimes called 'quality in perception'. Others see a direct link between quality and marketing, since quality is meaningless unless it refers to market perceptions (Davies and Scribbins, 1985: 5). In competitive markets, quality is seen as a vital tool for those organizations wishing to maintain a current market share or secure a competitive advantage (Green, 1994: 7). Indeed, Peters argues that 'every firm must ensure that quality is always defined in terms of customer perceptions' (Peters, 1989: 64). Middlehurst goes further in underlining the importance in educa-tion of the relationship between institutions and all stakeholders: 'In order to succeed in the delivery of quality outcomes, a range of different constituencies must be satisfied, from students and various groupings of professionals, to employers, funders and clients, community representatives, parents and society at large' (Middlehurst, 1992: 27).

The sheer range of these 'constituencies' can be confusing and challenging to edu-cational leaders and the balancing of the sometimes competing demands of students, parents, local and national agencies, can be one of the most difficult and time-consuming issues faced by educational professionals.

Concepts associated with quality: 'quality control' versus 'quality assurance'

The term 'quality' tends to be applied to all the activities associated with increasing performance. However, there is a wide range of associated concepts that can be confusing and which are quite frequently employed inappropriately or inaccurately.

Quality control is the oldest quality concept and involves the detection and elimination of components or final products which are not up to standard. It is an after-production process concerned with detecting and rejecting defective items. Quality control is usually carried out by quality professionals, known as quality controllers or inspectors, and inspection and testing are the most common methods of quality control and are widely used in education to determine whether standards are being met (Sallis, 2002: 19–20). Given that it is an after-the-event process, quality control is difficult to apply to educational settings since teaching and learning are continuous processes that operate in social settings and it is inadvisable, at best, to attempt to reject learning that has been inadequate in some way. Nonetheless, this concept does have some relevance, since if teaching and learning approaches are identified as being deficient steps can be taken to ensure more effective approaches in the future (Ellis, 1993: 5).

Quality assurance, commonly known as 'QA', is a term that has come into general usage in schools and colleges. It differs from quality control in that it refers to systematic approaches to prevent faults occurring in the first place. In this sense, quality assurance is a means of producing defect- and fault-free products by consistently meeting product specification or getting things right first time, every time. Crucially, quality assurance should be the responsibility of the workforce rather than the inspector, although inspection can have a role to play in quality assurance. The quality of the product or service is ensured by there being a system in place, known as a quality assurance system, which lays down exactly how production should take place and to what standards (Sallis, 2002: 19–20). This enables a manufacturer or producer to guarantee to a customer or client that the goods or service concerned will meet standards consistently (Ellis, 1993: 4). The attraction of such systems lies in the fact that they place the onus on workers to ensure high standards throughout and, in-line with the notions of Deming referred to earlier, preclude the requirement for inspection systems that may be expensive and intrusive. The key features of an effective quality assurance system are:

- an effective quality management system;
- periodic audit of the operation of the system;
- periodic review of the system to ensure it meets changing requirements.

(after Munro-Faure and Munro-Faure, 1992: 6–7)

In essence, quality control tells us that a product or service is wrong, quality assurance prevents it going wrong. The underlying principle is one of conformance to specification and management systems which allow this. The components of a management system to assure quality will include:

- clearly defined roles and responsibilities;
- documentation to formalize procedures;
- identification of customers' requirements;
- a quality policy;
- clear work instructions and process control;
- procedures for corrective action;
- management audit;
- inspection and testing.

(West-Burnham, 1994: 168–69)

Schools and colleges have increasingly addressed these issues, either because of an internal commitment to increasing effectiveness or because they have become statutory requirements of national policy. For instance, in England, schools experience the Office for Standards in Education (Ofsted) inspection regime, which will be discussed in detail later in this text. This would expect schools to have well-developed policies on a wide range of matters, apart from teaching and learning, such as behaviour management, relationships with the wider community and so on.

Quality management is the process whereby a particular organization is managed to assure quality, or, less ambiguously, 'the management of quality' (Ellis, 1993: 5). Thus quality management includes the collective plans, activities and events established to ensure that a product, process or service will satisfy given needs (Liston, 1999: 159).

Quality assessment involves the judgement of performance and outcomes against certain criteria or objectives, in order to establish whether the required standard has been achieved, and if failures or shortfalls occur, to ensure that they are corrected (Middlehurst, 1992: 28).

Quality audit involves 'evaluation to verify the effectiveness of control' (Liston, 1999: 159) and investigates whether an institution has appropriate quality assurance mechanisms in place and whether they are working effectively (Cox and Ingleby, 1997: 5).

Much of this text will focus on issues associated with inspection regimes and the term 'inspection' can itself be defined as 'an external, summative process judging the extent to which an organisation meets externally imposed criteria' (West-Burnham, 1994: 158). Two important and associated terms are 'monitoring', which involves 'the collection of data and evidence to inform other review activities' and 'quality review' which encompasses a range of management procedures which collect data to establish the extent to which intentions have been achieved (West-Burnham, 1994: 158).

We have noted that it is quite common to employ terms such as inspection, quality control, quality assurance and quality management loosely, especially in the context of education, but there is an argument that more precise definitions of these terms can be useful since the implications of each are very different (West-Burnham, 1995: 15). The relationship between these elements and their associated levels of management is revealed in Table 1.1.

If an organization is to move from inspection to quality management a number of significant culture changes take place. Increasing awareness and involvement of clients and suppliers is required and the personal responsibility of the workforce increases. There is increasing emphasis on process as well as product, within an imperative that

Table 1.1 Commonly employed terms and their meanings in practice

Inspection	Post-production review
	Re-working
	Rejection
	Control of workforce
	Limited to physical products
Quality Control	Concerned over product
	Responsibility with supervisors
	Limited quality criteria
	Some self-inspection
	Paper-based systems
Quality Assurance	Use of statistical process control
	Emphasis on prevention
	External accreditation
	Delegated involvement
	Audit of quality systems
	Cause and effects analysis
Total Quality Management	Involves suppliers and customers
	Aims for continuous improvement
	Concerns products and processes
	Responsibility with all workers
	Delivered through teamwork

Source: Based on West-Burnham, 1995; derived from Dale and Plunkett, 1991: 7.

emphasizes continuous improvement. This movement within the field is one of the reasons why the 'Total Quality Management' approach became popular in recent years and it is to this approach that we now turn.

Total Quality Management in education

Total Quality Management (TQM) became something of a vogue term during the 1990s. Not only does it incorporate quality assurance, it extends and develops it in order to create a quality culture where the aim of every member of staff is to please their customers, in an environment where the structure of their organization enables and encourages them to do so. It is about providing the customer with what they want, when they want it and how they want it and involves moving with changing customer expectations and fashions to design products and services that meet and exceed their expectations. The perceptions and expectations of customers will change over time, so organizations have to find ways of listening to their customers in order to be able to respond to their changing tastes (Sallis, 2002: 19–20). TQM is accomplished by a series of small-scale incremental projects. The Japanese use the term *kaizen* for this approach to continuous improvement. This is most easily translated as step-by-step improvement (Sallis, 2002: 29).

TQM has been said to offer a holistic approach to managing and improving institutions. It is not a panacea but it does offer some useful ideas which have the potential to enhance the quality of education. Marsh (1992: 44) offers the following definition: 'Total quality is a philosophy with tools and processes for practical implementation aimed at achieving a culture of continuous improvement driven by all the employees of an organization in order to satisfy and delight customers'.

West-Burnham argued that TQM has much to offer schools and colleges because it is value-driven, has a clear moral imperative and is customer-focused. In education this would mean that processes are driven by the needs of young people, parents and the community (1994: 172). This focus on customers is one of the central tenets of TQM. West-Burnham (1995) identifies four of the central principles of the customer focus within TQM theory:

1. Quality is defined by the customer not the supplier, e.g. lessons should be 'fit for purpose'.
2. Schools and colleges should be 'close to the customer' in that they meet their needs, e.g. parents' consultation arrangements should match the availability of parents rather than the convenience of teachers.
3. Quality schools and colleges 'know their customers' and take the trouble to find out their needs and preferences, e.g. parental or student surveys on aspects of school life.
4. Customer satisfaction may be determined by 'moments of truth': that is striking examples of good or poor quality. Thus quality consists in the experiences of the customer rather than the aspirations of the supplier.

The customer focus of TQM does not just involve meeting the requirements of external customers. Colleagues within the institution are also customers, and rely upon the internal services of others to do their job effectively. According to this approach, everyone working in a school, college or university is both a supplier and a customer of others, and each member of staff both gives and receives services. If one accepts this notion then internal customer relationships are vitally important if an institution is to function efficiently and effectively; the best way of developing the internal customer focus is to help individual members of staff to identify the people to whom they provide services. The people next in line are thus also direct customers, whether they are external to the institution or internal to it. The standards may be contractual, but they may also be negotiable. Notions of status and hierarchy do not enter into this relationship; the standard of service provided to someone junior in the institution is as important as the service provided to the Principal or the Chair of Governors (Sallis, 2002: 32). To clarify this further, Sallis (2002: 33) suggests the idea of internal marketing since, he suggests, it is the staff who make the quality difference. They produce successful courses and satisfied clients. Internal marketing is a useful tool for communicating with staff to ensure they are kept informed about what is happening in the institution and gives them the opportunity to feed back ideas. Simply, the idea of internal marketing is that new ideas, products or services have to be as effectively marketed to staff as they are to clients. Staff cannot convey the message of the institution to potential customers without proper product knowledge and an enthusiasm for the institution's aims. Internal marketing is a stage on from communicating ideas. It is a positive and proactive process which demands a commitment to keep staff informed and to listen to their comments.

The problem with business models of quality when applied to education

It is important to note that business models of quality such as TQM are not without their critics when applied to social organizations such as schools and colleges. For instance, there are those who offer a technical critique of this approach and suggest that TQM theorists give too little attention to differences between customers and their ability to influence the nature of services (Capper and Jamison, 1993: 28). West-Burnham (1994: 56–57) identifies a number of possible objections to TQM in the education service, based on the fact that education is a service rather than an industry. Moreover, as we have discussed, teaching has traditionally been perceived as a professional occupation with all that implies in terms of autonomy of decision-making; for this reason alone education and business models of quality may be viewed as inimical. Indeed, the employment of such commercial models has caused a debate about the nature of professionalism in education which remains unresolved. New forms of professional identity have been constructed to take account of the intrusion of these new approaches to quality (McCulloch *et al.*, 2000). Furthermore, the great emphasis placed on customer satisfaction that lies at the heart of TQM is inimical to education, since there has always been a problem in defining who education is for; the child, parent, society at large, or all of these constituencies. Indeed, for some, TQM is the final evidence of the notion that education has been bent to the will of the state and so provides final evidence of the concept of performativity noted earlier (Steingard and Fitzgibbons, 1993).

The problematic nature of these issues may be the reason why there has been less focus on TQM in education in recent years. Nonetheless, it is true to say that many of the main features of TQM models have become integral to school and college leadership and management. There are those who argue that TQM approaches are actually increasingly relevant in education in a period when globalization has caused a greater concentration on the competitiveness of education systems in terms of supplying the best-qualified work force to the economy (Mukhopadhyay, 2005). Indeed, there is now a wide range of quality assurance frameworks employed by schools and colleges in the UK, in addition to those embedded in statutory frameworks such as Investors in People, the Charter Mark, The National Healthy Schools Standard, and The Quality Mark, and educational leaders cannot ignore their relevance (NAHT, 2007: 114–16).

Conclusion

The main conceptual frameworks for quality management grew out of work in the business sector in the early and middle period of the twentieth century. Education was comparatively slow to adopt such concepts and it was not until the 1980s and 1990s that terms such as 'quality assurance' began to enter into the discourse associated with educational institutions. The reasons for this are complex and focus around the fact that schools, colleges and higher education institutions are social settings which cannot easily adopt ideas more readily associated with industrial production. However, the move towards local management of schools and colleges that has been evident across the developed world has meant that many educational institutions need to integrate management approaches that have proved themselves in the business sector. In so doing it is important to try to remove some of the conceptual confusion associated with quality regimes since there has been a tendency to employ terminology loosely in education.

Inevitably, there are those who continue to argue that quality models should have nothing to do with the social settings of schools and other educational organizations. It is undoubtedly true that the work of schools and colleges is centrally concerned with teaching and learning rather than with the creation of wealth, as is the case in industry. For this reason the adoption of quality management processes is no panacea for the problems that confront educational institutions. Nonetheless, the fact that quality systems have become an integral part of school systems across the world and the language of quality has become commonplace in educational settings cannot be ignored. For this reason it is important to reach shared understandings about the terms employed and how they relate to schools and colleges.

2   Accountability in education

Introduction

Chapter 1 introduced the concept of quality and this chapter will examine the relationship between quality, accountability, and leadership in terms of the responsibilities of leaders in educational organizations. There is nothing new about the notion of accountability in education. National inspectors were appointed from the early part of the nineteenth century, and external inspection of schools was an accepted part of education. At the same time, in the UK, North America and Europe, many technical institutes were founded which were accountable to the rapidly developing networks of local government and universities, or their precursor organizations. These technical institutes embodied a strong commitment to internal systems of quality, based on scholarship. As we shall see in this chapter this pattern was operant for much of the nineteenth and twentieth centuries. In more recent times new accountability systems have been developed which have both acknowledged the autonomy of educational institutions and, at the same time, accented their accountability to central government. It is only in the most recent of times that a balance has been struck which enables educational institutions to operate sophisticated internal review processes while at the same time being subject to external inspection.

This chapter will examine the process by which modern conceptions of accountability were reached in education. More specifically, it will explore:

- the origins of accountability regimes in education;
- definitions of accountability;
- quality standards in education and their relevance to accountability and inspection;
- the accountability of senior leaders to governors;
- accountability for the effectiveness and efficiency of educational organizations, prior to further exploration in Chapter 6.

We conclude by noting that the requirement to work within external quality frameworks and to be accountable to external inspection regimes has become commonplace and an accepted part of the role of educational leaders and teachers and that, although challenging, this is an area that can lead to significant improvements in learning and teaching. The discussion is based largely on the UK experience.

The origins of accountability regimes in education

The origins of state-managed external accountability systems in the UK can be traced back to the nineteenth century with the founding of Her Majesty's Inspectors (HMI) in 1839 (Maclure, 2001). For much of the twentieth century, however, the teaching profession was not considered to be accountable to central government for the content of the curriculum, nor was it required to justify its decisions to policy-makers or parents (Scott, 1999). However, as we began to explore in the previous chapter, whilst relatively independent from governmental and parental pressures, schools were in fact accountable to Local Education Authorities and to HMI, even though the latter's inspections were infrequent, with the usual time-frame considered to be one inspection every seven years. As noted earlier in this text, the accountability ethic during this period was, therefore, based on the professionalism of teachers and their relationship with pupils, parents, and Local Education Authority advisers and inspectors. As far as England and Wales are concerned, it was only with the arrival of the 1988 Education Reform Act that the principles of universalism and social equality were replaced with an ideology of the market based on individualism, public choice and accountability (Duncan, 2003) by establishing a National Curriculum, a national regime of testing, and a new external inspection system based around the creation of the Office for Standards in Education (Ofsted).

A similar centralizing dictum has been operant in further and higher education in England. For much of the twentieth century there was a bifurcation in accountability systems whereby charter universities, founded by royal assent, enjoyed relative autonomy from state control whilst further education colleges and polytechnics were locally accountable and had strong links to local authorities. The decades following the 1980s have witnessed the creation of a wide range of quality and accountability regimes based around organizations created by central government. For instance the Quality Assurance Agency for Higher Education exists to provide independent assessment of how higher education institutions in the UK maintain their academic standards and quality (QIA, 2009a). Meanwhile, the Quality Improvement Agency for Lifelong Learning (QIA) was set up to spark fresh enthusiasm for innovation and excellence in the further education and skills sector (QIA, 2009b) and the Learning Skills Network (LSN) has a role to enhance education and training by quality improvement and staff development programmes that support specific government initiatives, through research, training and consultancy; and by supplying services directly to schools, colleges and training organizations (LSN, 2009).

Since this dramatic shift in educational policy, accountability has dominated the political and public thinking in education in the UK and internationally – based on questions about relative performance and value for money. This discourse began by examining the effects of individual heads and principals, their styles, characteristics and approaches and the possible effects of their leadership upon the processes and outcomes of school, although increasingly it has extended to the leadership functions of teachers throughout educational institutions. This was based on the assumption that educational organizations would respond to public pressure and to the market choices that parents and students would make, once they were informed about the outcomes that individual institutions achieved. However, also emerging from this public and professional discourse has been the review of performance management and the development of research into how schools and colleges can be improved. The emergence of a debate on assessment processes has been given greater impetus by the creation of systems of metrics that analyse the value-added characteristics of educational institutions. Such metrics play an increasing role in accountability systems and impact on perceptions of a variety of issues related to school improvement, such as the correlation between the quality of teaching and the achievement of pupils and between the quality of learning and leadership.

The growing complexity of accountability frameworks and the increasing plethora of quality and accountability agencies has raised questions about the definition of the term 'accountability' in education and it is this problematic issue to which we turn next.

Definitions of accountability in an era of 'performativity'

The term accountability describes a relationship in which one party has an obligation, contractual or otherwise, to account for their performance of certain actions to another. The Nolan Committee encapsulated this with a definition which stated that: 'holders of public office are accountable for their decisions and action to the public and must submit themselves to whatever scrutiny is appropriate to their office' (Nolan Committee, 1997: 138). This comparatively simple, not to say simplistic, model has been challenged a number of times in recent years because of a growing realization that accountability takes different forms, contingent upon the nature of the organizations and the operant cultural norms.

It is ironic that increased accountability in education has been mirrored by significantly increased autonomy for schools. The arguments for the increased autonomy of schools from the LEA are similar to those directed at organizations in the business sector: those who are closest to the people or children know best what needs to be done. Educational managers are closer to the clients and better able than more remotely sited managers to identify the needs of the clients. In addition, managers will give primacy to satisfying clients' needs and will also know the best way of combining available resources to meet as many of these needs as possible. Finally, in making decisions on resource combinations, the unit manager will vary the proportion of different resources as production requires and make relative price changes (Thomas, 1997).

These arguments about improvements through increased organizational autonomy are part of a similar debate about the benefits of decentralization in all aspects of education, which affects schools, colleges and Local Authorities (LAs). With this greater level of autonomy and decentralization from local employers comes a need for senior managers to develop the requisite leadership and management competencies to act in this new environment. However, as organizations take on more autonomy they also become more accountable, since information is less distorted and feedback loops are shorter (Peters, 1992: 568). Kogan devised three models of accountability in education. First, public or state control, which entails the use of authority by elected representatives, appointed officials and the heads and others who manage schools. Second, professional control, which is control of education by teachers and professional administrators, a form of control that may include self-reporting evaluation. Third, consumerist control, which takes the form of participatory democracy and partnership in the public sector or market mechanisms in the private or partly privatized sector (Kogan, 1986: 24).

Halstead (1994) extended this model to suggest six dimensions which included: the central control model (contractual, employer dominant); the self-accounting model (contractual, professional dominant); the consumerist model (contractual, consumer dominant); the chain of responsibility model (responsive, employer dominant); the professional model (responsive, professional dominant); and, the partnership model (responsive, consumer dominant). Scott subsequently drew on this work to delineate five models of accountability, of which the most relevant to this text is *the evaluative state model* (Scott, 1999), which, as noted already in Chapter 1, is particularly applicable to state education systems in an era of performativity (Duncan, 2003).

As evidence of this we may note that in England the state gives over the precise implementation of policy to semi-independent bodies such as Ofsted which, whilst accountable to government ministers, override existing forms of accountability. In this model, the inspection process itself becomes the means by which schools comply with government policy (Lumby and Foskett, 1999: 27). In this accountability system the responsibility for failure shifts from the government to quasi-governmental bodies and the school or college or university itself. Such an approach has given rise to concerns that educational discourse has increasingly been dominated by a vocabulary that is itself dominated by government inspection agencies such as Ofsted (Ferguson *et al.*, 2000: 5).

More recent work has sought to shift the emphasis of accountability onto teaching and learning by giving increased prominence to concepts such as evaluation and assessment, which may be either internal or external to the organization. In this formulation evaluation is a process which involves looking back systematically at what has been accomplished and measuring the present position against the original aims (Coleman, 2005: 152). This change in emphasis mirrors the developing frameworks for accountability that will be discussed later in this text and which have placed great stress on self-evaluation processes and the importance of inspection in improving learning.

In fact, in just the same way that notions of professionalism have been forced to change over time so models of accountability have been transformed in recent decades to take account of the changing policy context. Indeed, systems of accountability are value-laden and can change, depending on the particular historical and political circumstances of the time. For example, since the beginning of the Ofsted accountability regime many schools have been forced to find ways of managing and controlling the inspection process in ways which better serve the interests of school staff, parents and pupils. Such schools have learned to use external accountability systems to their advantage as well as to improve and develop themselves (Duncan, 2003). This is a challenging viewpoint for many senior managers of schools, who can feel overwhelmed by the demands of government, not only in the amount of data being demanded by the centre but also by the legislative drive for schools to be more accountable and to make more information available to parents and governors about the performance of the individual child and the institution as a whole. Along with greater delegation and increased self-management comes the need for greater accountability, which is translated into the desire to measure progress against a range of performance indicators and to publish results.

Quality standards in education and their relevance to accountability and inspection

In England and Wales, the Education (Schools) Act 1992 led to the establishment of Ofsted which was given responsibility for the inspection of schools and, by 2005, had been requested to create an integrated framework for the inspection of educational organizations from pre-school to further education. The key characteristics of the original Ofsted model may be summarized as: all schools were to be inspected on a four-year cycle against a standardized inspection procedure with explicit criteria for inspection. A standardized report to governors was to be published with a summary to parents; there was also a requirement for an action plan to respond to the report's findings. The Act required inspectors to report on: the quality of the education provided by the school; the educational standards achieved in the school; whether the financial resources made available to the school are managed efficiently; and the spiritual, moral, social and cultural development of pupils at the school.

In the post-compulsory sector the Further Education Funding Council (FEFC) was given the responsibility for quality assessment in colleges of further education in England, on the basis of a *Framework for Validating Self-Assessment through Inspection* (FEFC, 1997). Subsequently, Ofsted took over this responsibility as part of the integrated framework noted earlier (Ofsted, 2005). From the outset colleges were required to carry out their own self-assessments according to guidelines published by the FEFC, with these assessments being validated through a process of external inspection. The guidelines required colleges to carry out self-assessments in the areas of the college mission; teaching and learning; students' achievements; curriculum content, organization and management; support for students; resources; quality assurance; management; and governance. Subsequent inspections are planned in consultation with the college and involve the evaluation of the college's own quality systems. This emphasis on a quality 'loop' that integrates internal assessment with external inspection has enabled colleges in the further education sector to identify overlapping and sometimes contradictory quality demands such as the imperatives to enhance achievement whilst increasing recruitment and retention (Lumby, 2001: 81).

In England and Wales, quality assurance in higher education is the responsibility of the Quality Assurance Agency for Higher Education (QAA). The purpose of the QAA was defined as: 'to provide an integrated quality assurance service for higher education institutions throughout the UK' (QAA, 2000: 1). The process involves 'subject reviews' where, each year, a number of subjects are reviewed on a rolling programme with a view to reviewing 'all HE provision'. The subject review method evaluates the quality of educational provision within a subject area, as defined by a unit of review, and is focused, at the level of the subject, on the quality of the student learning experience and student achievement (QAA, 2000: 7). The main features of the method are peer review, self-assessment, and review against the subject provider's aims and objectives.

It is notable that further and higher education accountability frameworks have been much swifter to integrate internal and external evaluation processes and it is only in comparatively recent years that the model operant in schools has encouraged self-review as a formal process.

The accountability of senior leaders to governors

Initially, when local financial management was introduced, educational institutions were anxious about financial controls, budgetary management and administrative arrangements, since educational leaders had to develop strategic processes that linked their financial planning to the improvement of teaching and learning through the successful management of innovation and change (Davies and Ellison, 1997). This was especially the case in the schools sector, where school leaders gained unprecedented levels of control over the financial and human resource functions of their organization (Burton and Brundrett, 2005: 126). Alongside these early developments in self-management or self-governance, changes in the culture of accountability also occurred in the form of parental choice, a focus upon the customer, setting benchmarks, defining fitness for purpose and aiming for continuous improvement. For this reason the role of governing bodies in schools was forced to change and new frameworks were established that defined more clearly the responsibilities of governors in relation to the management of schools (DfEE, 1998b; DfES, 2005b). Under this new framework heads and principals have a duty to advise and assist the governing body in discharging its function, but are accountable to the governing body for the overall running of the school and must carry out agreed policies. This form of direct accountability is the most straightforward type of relationship, since it is a condition in which individual role holders are liable to review and the application of sanctions if their actions fail to satisfy those to whom they are accountable (Kogan, 1986: 53).

Thus, a head or principal is directly responsible to the governing body since it has the power both to appoint and to dismiss him or her. There are however, a number of groups with which heads work, not in a directly accountable role, but in a working partnership or functional role. These include pupils, parents, staff, local employers, the Local Authority, the local community, Ofsted and the Department for Children, Schools and Families (DCSF). Nonetheless, in this section we consider the stakeholders to whom the head has a formal or contractual accountability, the governors. In doing so one must remember that parents and governors are frequently overlapping constituencies, since the governing bodies of all schools have places set aside for parents.

It is important to point out that every governing body operates differently, not only according to the type and phase of school, but also according to foundation documents or articles of governance which will delineate who is on the governing body. The governing body is responsible for determining the aims and overall conduct of the school. This includes deciding, with the head, how the school should develop in order to maintain and improve its standards of education. In discussion with the governing body, the head is responsible for formulating policies for their eventual approval. The head is also responsible for implementing these policies, managing and administering the school and organizing and operating the school's curriculum. The head provides information, advice and recommendations and the governors should treat this information with respect and use it with discretion (NAHT, 2007). The head is the lead professional in the school and is automatically an *ex-officio* member of the governing body and has a right to attend all meetings of the governing body. The head's role is to advise the governing body of the educational implications of the decisions they reach (NAHT, 2007: 105). Table 2.1 outlines the relative responsibilities of the head and the governing body, especially in relation to key areas such as finance and the curriculum.

The governing body has a legitimate role in monitoring the success (or otherwise) of the school's actions. All staff should see the governors as an integral part of the school, whose purpose is to ensure that the best decisions are made in the interests of the children.

Table 2.1 The division of responsibilities between the governing body and the headteacher or principal

The Headteacher/Principal	The Governing Body
Draws up the curriculum plan within the overall statutory framework and the policy framework set by the governing body;	Determines a policy for delivering a broad and balanced curriculum within the statutory framework in consultation with the headteacher, including a policy on sex education;
Ensures its implementation;	Satisfies itself that requirements for the delivery and assessment of the National Curriculum are being met and that Religious Education is being provided;
Is responsible for day-to-day decisions on the curriculum;	Ensures that appropriate monitoring arrangements are in place and that outcomes are being evaluated through reports from the headteacher;
Draws up the proposed budget options for – delegated funds; – special purpose grants; – other anticipated income for consideration and approval by the governing body;	Discusses and adopts the budget (with any amendments which are agreed);
Incurs expenditure within delegated limits, once the budget has been agreed;	Agrees limits of delegation and the power to transfer between budget headings (virement);
Submits regular monitoring reports of expenditure against budget to the governing body, or finance committee.	Monitors expenditure against budget and evaluates the outcome; These functions, apart from the approval of the budget, may be delegated to a finance committee where one exists to work with the headteacher.

Despite the fact that the head has legal accountability to the governors it must be noted that he or she has the prime responsibility for the children and young people in their care, although this accountability may often be exercised through the parents, or other responsible adults, as the legal guardians of the pupils. As students mature, accountability may be increasingly given over to them directly, particularly after they reach the age of 18 years. Ofsted and OHMCI (Wales) evaluate and report on how well the governors, head and staff with management responsibilities contribute to the education provided by the school and the standards achieved by all of its pupils by examining the extent to which the leadership and management produce an effective school that promotes and sustains improvement in educational standards achieved and the quality of the education provided (DfES, 2004a; Ofsted, 1995, 2003a).

Accountability for the effectiveness and efficiency of educational organizations

One of the most important aspects of school autonomy is the consideration of whether or not the available money is used effectively and efficiently; it has been argued that it is in this area where there is scope for leadership, vision and lateral thinking (Downes, 1997). In England, the *National Standards for Headteachers* indicate that heads account for the efficiency and effectiveness of the school to the governors and to others, including pupils, parents, staff, local employers and the local community (DfES, 2004a). In pursuance of this requirement heads must provide information, objective advice and support to the governing body to enable it to meet its responsibilities for securing effective teaching and learning, improved standards of achievement and for achieving efficiency and value for money.

The generally accepted definition of an effective school is one in which pupils progress further than might have been predicted from consideration of the attainment of its intake (Institute of Education, 2003). However, effectiveness is also about whether the school achieves its aims and objectives for all of its pupils, in order to raise student achievement. The efficient school achieves high outcomes for its pupils at the minimum cost; it wastes none of its financial resources and derives the maximum benefit from what it already has, in order to achieve value for money. Skilful management of both the internal and external financial and resource boundaries are key competencies of senior managers and have become a major aspect of accountability for senior leaders in education. However, it is clear that the two aspects of effectiveness and efficiency cannot be viewed in isolation from each other. Therefore, educational leaders must review data arising from the monitoring of both the financial and educational outcomes of the organization. In order to do this they will need to examine closely whether financial and educational targets are being met and the planning of both these areas must be integrated. In this sense, whatever standpoint is adopted, under the current regime of devolved management operant in many developed nations, schools and colleges must be managed as businesses (Keating and Moorcroft, 2006).

Conclusion

Accountability and inspection are nothing new in education but the last three decades have witnessed a new framework for education that integrates many of the elements of quality frameworks from broader management theory. For some in education this is anathema, but for leaders of schools, colleges and universities the requirement to work within external quality frameworks and to be accountable to external inspection regimes has become commonplace and an accepted part of their role. There is evidence that many educational leaders find this element of their work the most challenging that they have to face (Coleman, 2005: 164). No doubt this is, in part, because senior leaders in particular are held responsible for the performance of their organizations. However, accountability in education is particularly problematic since school leaders are held to account by such a wide range of stakeholders. This issue will be addressed in greater detail as the text unfolds.

3 The process of developing a culture of quality

Introduction

A key focus of this chapter is an exploration of the role of leadership in establishing an organizational culture conducive to increased quality and organizational improvement which is reflected by enhanced learner outcomes. Leaders need to know the influences of the existing cultural conditions, the kind of culture they wish to establish and how the existing culture needs to be modified to achieve these aims. Such insights may not be easily accessible or lend themselves to easy definition in some organizations and in the skill set of some leaders. Leaders attempting to modify culture need to have a critical awareness of how quality enhancement can be supported culturally, as well as structurally, if improvement efforts are to flourish and be sustained. If improving quality is equated to doing what you do better, so that learners' and other stakeholders' needs are served to a higher standard, then leading and managing quality points to the fundamental requirement of building quality enhancement systems from the ground up. This is a challenging task and implies that leadership action can foster a culture of quality by forging shared organizational values and priorities. Such action is likely to involve securing a shared focus on improvement, systematic information gathering, consultation, individual and institutional learning, shared decision-making, collaboration, teacher professionalism and trust so that improved practices and processes can lead to improved outcome, reflecting high standards within the educational market place. In this chapter we seek to define the term culture and to explore links between leadership and the development of a culture of quality. In so doing we explore:

- culture, quality and ethos;
- leadership, learning communities and cultural change;
- leadership, developing a culture of quality and school improvement;
- leadership, developing a culture of quality and improvement in the further and higher education sectors.

The chapter then concludes with a summary of the issues raised and points to key tenets in cultural management related to change, improvement and the raising of standards.

Culture, climate and ethos

The concept of culture is difficult to define (Sparkes, 1991; Schein, 1997; Prosser, 1999) and is usually explained in terms of the resultant symbols, rituals and interpersonal interactions that emerge when the prevailing values and beliefs of organizational members are played out in everyday working life. Giddens (1984) suggests that cultures are therefore social structures, reflective of the values and beliefs of members. The prevailing culture within an organization places both explicit and implicit requirements upon members to behave in particular ways in particular circumstances. Emphasizing both internal and external influences upon culture, Cray and Mallory (1998) suggest that practices in an organization are to a large extent fashioned by a combination of the mix of cultures represented in society, an individual's own cognitive frameworks, and the culture of the organization itself. The importance placed on this mix of cultures represented in society has led to the notion of cross-cultural theory which emphasizes that leaders need to understand the 'rules' by which people operate (Coleman and Earley, 2005). This knowledge is likely to be particularly important where teams or other organizational sub-sets are composed of people from two or more cultural backgrounds. In international schools, for example, it has been suggested that the health of a school's culture is dependent upon all staff being interculturally literate (Poore, 2005).

The research literature frequently refers to organizational culture as a 'single entity'. Deal and Kennedy (1988) offer an analysis of the formation of a 'single entity' organizational culture and identify the following components:

a.   shared values and beliefs;
b.   heroes and heroines;
c.   ritual;
d.   ceremony;
e.   stories;
f.   an informal network of cultural players.

However, organizational cultures, in reality, may not be merely one homogeneous entity and sub-groups within organizations, such as departments or groups of learners, may well bring to prominence their own values and beliefs and establish sub-cultures (Sarason, 1982; Stoll and Fink, 1996) which contribute to an overall prevailing culture. Indicating the input of sub-groups to prevailing culture, Staessens and Vandenberghe (1994) suggest the likelihood of a shared culture in many schools, jointly owned by staff and students. In a study in four urban middle schools, Shann (1999) reported that sub-groups of learners saw overall culture as an amalgam of their relationships with peers and with staff and that these relationships were reflected in student behaviour patterns. The overall strength of the prevailing organizational culture will thus result in the broad acceptance of behavioural compliance by the majority of its members or may encourage individual or sub-group autonomy and dissonance (see Busher, 2006). The concept of the culture of an organization may be considered at one level as a single entity or at another level as a jig-saw of sub-cultures.

This 'slippery concept' of culture (McMahon, 2001) is made less clear in the literature by authors' interchangeable usage of the terms 'culture', 'climate' and 'ethos'
(Glover and Coleman, 2005; McLaughlin, 2005; Solvason, 2005). One view is that the
term 'climate' describes the shared assumptions that make up school culture (Heck
and Marcoulides, 1996: 83). 'Climate, therefore, is used in a more narrow sense to
describe teachers' perceptions of "how things are" on a day-to-day basis', whereas
'ethos' can be considered to emerge directly from the school's culture:

> The ethos of a school . . . is the unique, pervasive atmosphere or mood of the
> organization which is brought about by activities or behaviour, primarily in the
> realm of social interaction and to a lesser extent in matters to do with the envi-
> ronment, of members of the school, and recognized initially on an experiential
> rather than a cognitive level.
>
> (Allder, 1993: 69)

The present chapter seeks an understanding of culture in schools, colleges and
higher education institutions as a basis for enhancing quality and improving
learner outcomes. As such, two definitions of culture seem most apt. First, Glover
and Coleman (2005: 266) explain culture as: 'the integration of environmental,
organisational and experiential features of "school" existence to offer a context
for teaching and learning and its subsequent improvement'. Second, Ebbutt (2002:
125) describes culture as: '. . . a constellation of both written and unwritten expectations, values, norms, rules, laws, artefacts, rituals and behaviours that permeate a
society and influence how people behave'. It is these understandings of culture in
relationship to quality and improvement that will be drawn upon in the present
chapter.

Leadership, learning communities and cultural change

In seeking to create a prevailing culture that fosters shared organizational values,
expectations and behaviours most likely to offer a unity of focus on the improvement
of teaching and learning, improved student outcomes and an improved response to all
stakeholders' needs, incumbent leadership will require the engagement and involvement of as many organizational members as possible in order to deliver these aims.
Organizational leaders are likely to be influenced in their overall improvement efforts
by central government interventions intended to secure improvement. In the UK, for
example, a backdrop of policy-driven initiatives including the prescription of standards, enhanced self-management opportunities, organizational restructuring, professional development of staff and statutory interventions such as literacy development,
have underlain pressure and support by central government intended to raise the quality of teaching and learning in classrooms and, hence, standards in schools and colleges. Within individual organizations themselves, leadership actions to develop a
culture of quality receptive to continuous improvement are likely to include efforts to
secure willing staff involvement in planning, policy formation, a shared focus on
teaching and learning, teamwork and systematic self-review. It is also likely that efforts

to support the emergence of enhanced collaboration, trust and job satisfaction will include opportunities for professional learning, a greater standardization of processes and the modelling of required standards and expectations by incumbent leaders themselves. The efficacy of the structural and cultural evolution of educational organizations as learning organizations and the creation of learning communities within these organizations has been increasingly emphasized within the literature. A relationship between the professional learning of employees and 'continuous' improvement has been established in commercial organizations for many years. The importance of leadership commitment to professional learning as a lever to organizational improvement is reviewed by Jackson and Payne (2002).

The literature from the field of 'learning organizations' reveals that leaders are stimulators (who get things started); they are story tellers (to encourage dialogue and aid understanding); they are networkers and problem solvers too. They tend to have a wider social repertoire than has been customary in hierarchical educational settings, in order to encourage openness and to foster and support relationships during times when members are wrestling with ambiguity. They will build trust. They will model improvisation and be comfortable with risk-taking and spontaneity. They will also care, deeply, about teachers and children and about education, because that is the source of emotional energy for others. As leaders, they will place priority on the school as a context for adult learning. They will support staff at all levels to be able to 'make more sense of, and interpret, the emerging circumstances of school improvement' (Jackson and Payne, 2002: 4).

The interest and debate about schools and other educational organizations developing as learning communities has been associated with the possibility of a variety of benefits, including gains in outcomes for learners (Cochran-Smith and Lytle, 1999; Roberts and Pruitt, 2003). These benefits will be further explored in Chapter 5. In the schools sector, DuFour (2004) suggests that professional learning communities reflect three key components: collaborative work among the school's professionals; a strong and consistent focus on teaching and learning with that collaborative work; and the collection and use of assessment and other data for shared inquiry into performance over time. Moreover, research has shown that such improvement benefits based on learning community activity can be realized. For example, in a study of mathematics education in a case-study school in the US, Lieberman (2009) suggested that staff participation in a learning community helped establish the behavioural norm of becoming more innovative and also more enquiring about ways to serve students better. This research also showed that participation in a learning community helped teachers to better embrace the notion of continual improvement. Effective professional learning communities appear to take collective responsibility for staff and student learning and are capable of engendering shared values and vision, openness, inclusion and mutual trust and support. The inclusion of the voices of stakeholders, including staff and student voice, are thought to have much potential for improving teaching and learning within such communities.

In seeking to foster cultural change in educational organizations that enables the development of characteristics of learning communities, incumbent leaders will need to take stock of the current prevailing culture within their organization and assess what actions may be needed in order to enable improvement to take place. This is made difficult by the fact that the existing prevailing culture is very likely to be influential in stakeholder expectations of the behaviour of incumbent leaders. Moving away from the established norms may be uncomfortable for some staff, and questions of the acceptability of change may emerge. For this reason, given that cultures are deep-rooted, plans to change an organization's culture could be difficult and possibly detrimental to the fabric of the organization (Solvason, 2005). This gives rise to the question as to whether leadership can actually influence the prevailing culture or sub-cultures within an organization and, if so, how leaders sustain or change the core values and beliefs of organizational members. Indeed, Donnelly (2000) questions whether cultural change is something that can be aimed for, or is something that emerges through interactions within the organization.

Alvesson (1993) suggests that leaders are able to modify the prevailing culture, but their actions are also constrained by it. For example leaders may seek to establish greater collegiality as an alternative to inflexible hierarchy, thus encouraging greater collaboration and trust between stakeholders. However, influences from external sources such as local community culture and internal sources such as a mosaic of resistant sub-cultures may make attempts to change or modify culture very difficult, if changes are to be at least acceptable to the majority of members. The larger the number of sub-cultures the more difficult change is likely to be. Notwithstanding these concerns, in their more optimistic analysis, Hall and George (1999) unequivocally suggest that the impact of leadership upon culture is detectable throughout the school and Lam *et al.* (2002) isolate leadership attitude as a feature determining culture. Given that leaders are exemplars of the values and beliefs that underpin organizational culture, they can set the tone for how members of staff are expected to behave. It has been suggested that culture cannot be controlled, but may be influenced by those able to exert power, authority or influence within the organization. For example, the principal can exert power but this may be countered if enough people are working in contradiction (Lumby, 2001). Leaders are attributed with the task of helping to create an organizational culture that will foster organizational learning (Schein, 1997), however, Lakomski (2001) cautions that the leaders themselves are also part of the organizational culture and will, therefore, have difficulty stepping out of it when required by circumstance. It is clear that leadership can shape the work contexts of staff (Evans, 2001) and in so doing can promote the cultural elements of equity, justice, interpersonal relations and collegiality. In summary, it is suggested that leaders do have the wherewithal to make interventions that can help secure movement towards a culture of quality.

The role of leadership in developing a culture of quality and school improvement

The importance of effective leadership in schools and its direct relationship to the quality of education experienced by students is well-established (DfES, 2004a; Bell *et al.*, 2003; Leithwood and Riehl, 2003; Southworth, 2004; Rutherford, 2005). A document presented to the UK Parliament by the Secretary of State for Education and

Skills (DfES, 2005b) emphasized that good leadership is at the heart of every good school. There has also been an increasing commitment to the distribution of leadership as a means of building leadership capacity and supporting school improvement (Gronn, 2000; Gronn, 2003a, 2003b; Harris, 2003, 2004; Muijs and Harris, 2003; DfES, 2004c; Hargreaves and Fink, 2006). It has been established that in most countries effective leaders exercise an indirect but powerful influence on the effectiveness of the school and on the achievement of students (Muijs and Harris, 2003).

A variety of possible prevailing of school cultures and influences upon culture have been described in the literature. For example, Handy (1993) relates organizational culture to leadership style and Hargreaves (1995) characterizes school culture as the balance between social control and social cohesion. Famously, Stoll and Fink (1996) suggest that school culture is related to the achievement of desired outcomes and characterize a four-fold typology:

a.   Moving (effective and improving organizations).
b.   Cruising (effective, but declining organizations).
c.   Struggling (ineffective and improving organizations).
d.   Sinking (ineffective and declining organizations).

Although this analysis is now some years old, more recent work continues to support similar typologies; the importance of creating a positive school culture supportive of change is highlighted by Muijs *et al.* (2004), who consider the improvement of schools in socioeconomically disadvantaged areas. Positive school culture is explained as reflecting open communication, coherence, high expectations and success stories. Open communication is reflective of a collaborative and distributive leadership style and has been found to characterize improving and effective schools in a number of studies (Harris and Chapman, 2001). The importance of positive staff relationships in bringing about improvement in urban schools is also emphasized by Ainscow and West (2006), who found that in schools in special measures seeking improvement, staff relationships could be fractured resulting in poor levels of collaboration. High levels of staff turnover in such schools can detract from the establishment of a positive culture due to difficulty in establishing a shared and stable vision. In order to bring about quality improvement teachers need the support of leadership and to believe that their actions will lead to improvement. Lack of such belief may result in continued poor collaboration and resistance to organizational change. Kennewell *et al.* (2000) argue that school leaders are the most influential actors in defining the culture and organization of their schools; however, they point out that the task of creating a more collaborative culture will need outstanding skills and resilience on the part of leaders in the face of possible staff division and conflict. Establishing more positive relationships among colleagues represents one pathway to a 'moving' (improving) school (Rosenholtz, 1989; Stoll and Fink, 1996).

Others have gone beyond the single dimension of culture and Hargreaves (2001) emphasizes the importance of both cultural and structural components of the 'social capital' required for school improvement. He suggests that the cultural aspect is associated with trust, while the structural aspects are based on the networks in which people are located. Structural change may take the form of the lessening of hierarchies to foster communication and collaboration. In schools in urban and challenging circumstances the promotion of higher levels of social capital, perhaps through more leadership distribution, is seen as important in school improvement and as a move towards a more risk-taking culture and the potential for sustainable improvement (Chapman, 2004). The transformation of culture, or the leadership of re-culturing as Fullan (2001) suggests, involves growing the capacity to seek, assess, select and incorporate new ideas and practices. The importance of cultural change in supporting other change intended to result in school improvement has been recognized in an Italian study (Paletta and Vidoni, 2006) and in a US study it has been recognized that successful school reform begins with unlocking the school's existing culture in advance of attempts to make changes (Weller, 1998). In a more recent study, Tondeur *et al.* (2009) found that structural characteristics, such as infrastructure and support, and cultural characteristics, such as leadership and innovativeness, are both relevant catalysts for change, an example being ICT integration in the classroom. This research showed that the more innovative the prevailing culture, the better the school's ability to tackle the structural changes needed to foster a change such as ICT integration into classrooms. Importantly the study also showed a reverse effect, indicating that if infrastructure does not allow teachers to use new technologies then greater innovativeness will be stifled.

Ensuring staff learning through knowledge-creating activities is an important means by which leaders can create the capacity for organizational improvement. Leaders can foster teachers' learning with and from other teachers in the interests of students. Effective leaders seek to empower staff by developing a culture of collaboration (Day *et al.*, 2001). Harris and Lambert (2003a, 2003b) also emphasize the role of leaders in capacity-building for improvement and suggest the importance of the creation of learning environments in which all staff can share in the distributed learning and improvement efforts:

> Effective school leaders build the capacity for improvement within their schools. They generate the conditions and create the climate for improvement to be initiated and sustained. Effective leaders orchestrate rather than dictate improvement and create learning communities within their schools. The role of leadership in school improvement is primarily to act as a catalyst in creating a learning environment for both teachers and pupils. This necessarily involves building the capacity within the school for learning and improvement to take place. Schools that 'build capacity' for implementing change are more likely to sustain improvement over time. In other words, they are able to generate both the readiness to change and the internal capacity to manage the change process.
>
> (Harris and Lambert, 2003a: 64)

The creation of a culture in which open networking between colleagues enables better staff relationships, mutual support and reflection has been shown to be important in the effective management of professional development cultures in schools (Law and Glover, 1996). However, not all schools benefit from the presence of such a prevailing culture (Law, 1999). In educational organizations, leadership and management teams should consider whether staff collaboration is facilitated or hindered by the professional development culture they have promoted. Indeed, Glover and Coleman (2005), drawing on the work of Reeves and Forde (2004), suggest that continuing professional development (CPD) is itself a factor affecting cultural change and development and could well promote cultural change because it may involve group formation and enhance staff relationships within these groups.

In a recent US study carried out to explore the effects of school culture and climate on student achievement, MacNeil *et al.* (2009) suggest that schools which were enabled to develop 'healthy learning environments' allowed students to achieve higher scores on standardized tests. Such 'health scores' are increased by principals promoting a strong vision for the school and establishing clear goals that are accepted and supported by staff. Leadership action has been seen to be influential in creating effective learning cultures in a variety of schools. For example, in a study of 11 secondary schools in the UK (Glover and Law, 2004), students were judged to be more successful where leadership was characterized by clarity of role and the delegation of tasks in the implementation of a vision for the school.

> Such schools appear to know where they are going and staff members implement policies to put themselves, and students under pressure to improve. Such an improving philosophy leads to generally integrated staff relationships with awareness of teams and social interaction to secure agreed objectives. This atmosphere appears to promote curriculum experimentation and deeper understanding of teaching and learning processes. As a result, students appreciate the planning and progression in their work, the variation of teaching approach to meet individual learning need, and the positive nature of staff–student relationships.
>
> (Glover and Law, 2004: 229)

James *et al.* (2006) contend that school cultures able to encourage successful learning are those which are strong, coherent and inclusive. Creating a culture allowing the school curriculum to be more accessible and inclusive for all pupils has been put forward as being central to school improvement (Busher, 2006). Such schools are aware of inclusion issues and take measures to encourage the engagement of all learners, as their outcomes can be strongly influenced by other factors such as family socioeconomic level and home environment. The idea of developing a sense of community within a school so that relationships become supportive of teaching and learning has been strongly advocated by Sergiovanni (1992, 2001). One way to foster such inclusion is to develop behaviour policies understood and accepted by both pupils and staff (Osler *et al.*, 2000).

Schools exist within a complex social context, but if individual leaders in an organization were to address all the challenges posed by the social contexts of learners, it would potentially be overwhelming. This challenge needs to be shared across and beyond the school via work with the community, community organizations and other professionals, and with parents. Enhancing the role of other professionals, paraprofessionals and the community within the school is likely to have an impact upon the prevailing school culture. The *Every Child Matters* (2003) agenda in the UK recognizes that schools have a critical role in raising the educational achievement of pupils in care and other groups who have consistently underachieved. This requires school leaders to collaborate well with other agencies to secure the delivery of internal and external support services. Multi-agency teams will need to find ways of working together and will perhaps share the same aspirations, with a focus on quality improvement as a means to secure improved learner outcomes.

Finally, the notion of becoming a 'learning-centred' organization denotes those educational organizations which have elected to place both student and staff learning at the core of their work. Linkages between leadership and learning are reflected in the learning of leaders themselves and, importantly, in their leadership actions that enable the learning of others (Swaffield and MacBeath, 2009). In short, a key role of senior leaders is to enable teachers to perform well with learners, so that they may make a strong contribution to high-quality teaching and learning. Such leadership requires the establishment of both structural and cultural support to enable the necessary capacity to address the changes needed within the contexts and communities in which these improvements are pursued. The inclusion of student voice has recently come to prominence within the literature as a means of establishing learners' experience of teaching and learning as a basis for quality improvement. Including students' voices in decision-making may assist those struggling to avoid disaffection and improve cooperation and mutual trust between them and other learners and teachers (Angus, 2006). The creation of more enabling relationships and inclusion could also support rises in student self-esteem, self-discipline, self-expression and interpersonal skills (Fielding, 2006). These gains are of value to all learners and strongly point to a place for student voice in learning-centred leadership and in leadership for learning itself. Leadership for learning and the place of student voice in organizational improvement is explored in much greater depth in Chapter 5.

Leadership, developing a culture of quality and improvement in the further and higher education sectors

In contrast to the schools sector, and despite the size and importance of the further education sector (the learning and skills sector), comparatively little research has been carried out with respect to the relationship between leadership, culture and improvement. It is, however, reasonable to assume that some of the key tenets may be transferred, perhaps with modification, between the school and the further and higher education sectors. Hodkinson and Bloomer (2000a) have suggested that the institutional culture of colleges has a significant impact upon students' disposition towards learning. Briggs (2005) highlights the ongoing and considerable changes to the environment within which sixth form colleges operate. Incorporation, curricular changes, new systems of funding and accountability represent some of the main drivers of change. Internally, such changes have led to greater diversity in provision and to change in the amalgam of staff and student culture. This author reports that there is a strong academic tenor associated with many sixth form colleges. Indeed, there is wariness on the part of some vocational students about the 'advanced' level elitism of such colleges. Against this background of emphasis on academic success, a cultural shift has become apparent in some colleges. This shift is characterized by tension between staff intent on maintaining the work ethic among students and the day-to-day reality of 16- to 19-year-old learners, who take for granted that full-time study is combined with part-time paid work and with leisure activities external to the college. Rustemier (1999) has highlighted the complexity of the notion of inclusion in some colleges and concludes that while some colleges claim to be working towards 'inclusiveness', the conceptualization of that inclusiveness easily co-exists with processes of exclusion. In the context of cultural change, inclusion and intended improvement, it is important to refer to the recent government directives in England aimed at ensuring cooperation between schools, colleges and work-based training providers, so that opportunities are created for all young people via high-quality and personalized vocational as well as academic pathways. This legislation required secondary schools to collaborate with changes to the 14–19 curriculum and qualifications structure, and includes changes intended to effect 14–16 re-engagement of those who may have become disaffected with their experience of school. Also, within the UK further education sector, inclusion of student voice and participation is becoming well-established as a contributor to quality improvement (LSC, 2006). Whilst suggesting that student voice has an important role to play in fostering improved learner engagement and pro-activity, Collinson (2007) rightly identifies that student empowerment can have implications for leadership and points out that the complex relationship between learning and leadership in this sector remains largely unexplored.

Originally undertaken in the 1990s, a typology of four models of university culture was proposed (see Table 3.1).

Examination of this typology reveals the presence of elements pertinent to quality frameworks in higher education. The models show that students may be portrayed as customers, evaluation data may be used to inform decision-making and standards may be used to indicate quality within the market place. Strydom *et al.* (2004) have examined trends in quality assurance within South African higher education and Van der

Table 3.1 Four possible models representing university cultures

Collegium	*Bureaucracy*
Decision-making is consensual	Decision-making is rule-based
Management style is permissive	Style based on standard procedures
Students seen as apprentice academics	Students are statistics
Evaluation is by peer review	Evaluation based on audit procedures
International community sets standards	Regulatory body sets standards
Enterprise	*Corporation*
Decision-making is flexible	Decision-making is political and tactical
Style is one of devolved leadership	Style is charismatic and commanding
Students are partners	Students are customers
Evaluation based on achievement	Evaluation based on performance indicators
Standards related to market strength	Standards related to institutional goals

Source: Modified after McNay, 1995 and Nauffal, 2004.

Westhuizen and Fourie (2002) have reviewed quality assurance systems in the US, Europe, UK and Australia. These authors suggest that the purpose of quality assurance systems includes the improvement of current practices, the need to meet the demands of public accountability, the need to demonstrate compliance with government goals for rationalization and use of targeted resources. They also identify that the primary data collection methods used in higher education quality assurance include self-evaluation, external peer-evaluation, statistical benchmarking and the standardization of practices. The introduction of quality assurance systems is impacting upon higher education organization cultures around the world (Strydom *et al.*, 2004). Changes in the UK higher education sector have been prompted by an increase in external regulatory mechanisms such as the Research Assessment Exercise (RAE), inspections by the Office for Standards in Education (Ofsted), and teaching quality assessments undertaken by the Quality Assurance Agency (QAA). Aligned with these frameworks, internal systems-based quality frameworks acknowledge the advent of increased levels of market accountability as institutions consider their reputations in the competition for both students and funding based upon their teaching and research performance. In the late 1990s, at an international level, the Bologna Declaration encouraged higher education organizations to cooperate in quality assurance, allowing student mobility and mutual recognition of qualifications. Discussions emanating from this declaration led to a call for universities to create internal quality cultures and develop standards and guidelines for quality assurance in the European Higher Education Area (ENQA, 2005). However, creating a culture of quality raises issues pertaining to transnational agreements on what this means. Gvaramadze (2008) describes a quality culture approach as being composed of quality as 'enhancement' with a focus on institutional and programme improvement and quality as 'transformation' where university staff and students seek to enhance learning experiences and place students at the centre of learning.

It is inevitable that the introduction of quality management systems has fundamental implications for institutional culture and that a culture of compliance is required in order that such systems may be introduced, operated and result in visible reporting. Although few would deny that accountability is proper within publicly funded organizations, there may be tensions between such systems and the professional and academic autonomy traditionally afforded in some universities. It has been evidenced that an over-emphasis on compliance and accountability can lead to an 'alienating culture' that is to the detriment of higher education (Hargreaves and Christou, 2002; Hodson and Thomas, 2003). There are concerns that the adoption of certain 'managerial styles' in some universities have the potential to create significant demoralization within the sector (Earley, 1994) and it has been suggested that the roles of some manager-academics in higher education require their adherence to the values of overt managerialism and performativity (see Deem and Brehony, 2005). The growth of the UK university sector since 1992 has seen the introduction of new or 'statutory' universities (former polytechnics and colleges of higher education) drawn from a more bureaucratic and potentially more managerialistic hierarchical local authority tradition which is in contrast to the tradition of the more collegial old universities (see Deem, 1998; Farnham, 1999). Although old universities have, necessarily, adopted cultures increasingly accepting of the need for internal and external quality frameworks, departments located within chartered and statutory universities may still have very different cultures, organizational structures and approaches to leadership and management (Smith, 2002, 2005).

As in other educational organizations, the prevailing culture of individual universities, their values, politics and stakeholders are very likely to influence practice. These practices will be guided, monitored and evaluated according to established internal and external quality frameworks. For example, efforts to improve the quality of teaching experienced by students has led to an increasing use of student satisfaction surveys and the incorporation of student voice captured via staff and student consultation committees. There is now much evidence of the use of student voice to inform improved academic integration and learning experiences (see Rhodes and Nevill, 2004; Campbell and Li, 2008) so as to enhance possibilities for better progression, retention and academic success. In some institutions the vestiges of tension between public and market accountability and the professional autonomy of academics still remains. The overwhelming trend however is towards ongoing cultural change and the universal establishment and adherence to internal quality management systems to ensure the best possible standing with respect to externally assessed quality data that will emerge in the public domain. The strategic and tactical approaches adopted by institutions are becoming far more developed and sophisticated in ensuring the best possible outcomes in response to such quality audits. It has been suggested that an over-reliance on tactics to ensure successful outcomes in external evaluations of quality are unlikely to build institutional or system-wide cultures of quality and continuous improvement (Gordon, 2002). Overall, the development and management of quality cultures that will lead to practices and processes focused on enhancement rather than on compliance are likely to find better acceptance within the higher education sector (Hodson and Thomas, 2003).

Conclusion

The 'slippery' concept of a prevailing organizational culture is thought potent in impacting upon how people within an organization behave and offers a context that may be facilitative or hindering to quality improvement, teaching and learning, and learner outcomes. Research has shown that many educational organizations have structures that may be regarded as 'the physical manifestation of the culture of the organisation' (Bush, 2003: 36). For example, a rigid hierarchical structure may reflect very formal relations. Therefore, a change in organizational structure and roles can have an impact on modifying the prevailing culture. Changing the prevailing culture can be difficult and raises questions pertaining to the nature of such a culture and how can it be created. Developing a culture of quality either within individual educational organizations or on a sector-wide or a system-wide basis has been linked with shared behaviours that maintain a focus on quality improvement and lead to attendant improvement in teaching and learning, student outcomes and closer attention to meeting the needs of all stakeholders. It is true that changes in organizational structure can enable teachers to talk more, collaborate and improve communication. However, structural change without attendant cultural change is likely to be limiting if leaders do not also build the capacity of teachers to change their behaviours in ways which support improvement activities. Leadership actions aimed at developing a culture receptive to continuous improvement are likely to include broad stakeholder involvement in planning; policy formation; a shared focus on teaching and learning; teamwork; and systematic self-review. It has been shown that one way in which leaders can act to modify prevailing culture and hence facilitate quality improvement is by changing how they work with their colleagues. The creation of open communication, professional learning, learning communities and networking can lead to the active development of a positive culture rather than accepting the so-called toxic cultures which resist change and improvement (McLaughlin, 2005; Solvason, 2005). When core values are understood and accepted by staff, the leader does not need to be physically present for staff teams to run effectively and it is possible that improvements can become sustainable (Hargreaves and Fink, 2006). In a recent small-scale study within a progressive independent school it was shown that autonomy, based on a highly developed sense of professional responsibility and accountability could co-exist. For these teachers, a view of professional accountability did not have to rely on the imposition of structures 'from above' (Warwick and Cunningham, 2006).

In the schools sector, the creation of learning communities has been associated with cultural change and improvement. Such communities enable a focus on the improvement of teaching and learning mostly enabled by the professional learning of staff themselves. The facilitation of professional learning is not the sole prerogative of heads of schools and in some organizations, such leadership for learning can involve empowering middle leaders and teachers to take a direct lead in teaching and learning within a collaborative culture (Fitzgerald and Gunter, 2006; Frost 2008). Chapter 8 of this book discusses in detail the notion that self-evaluation can constitute an important basis for quality improvement effort. Wroe and Halsall (1999) advocate a self-critical community approach to self-evaluation for improvement. They suggest that features associated with a professional learning community would assist in facilitating self-evaluation, enable the assertion of teacher autonomy through reflection on their own practices, and provide the empowerment to change these using their own professional judgement. Whilst little research has been undertaken in the further education sector with respect to the development of quality cultures, the adoption of student voice in improvement efforts has become increasingly well developed. The adoption of student voice is a feature also increasingly well developed in the higher education sector. The linkage of organizational outcomes in quality audits to the public domain, where market accountability can have significant positive or negative implications for educational organizations across all sectors, remains a potent spur for leaders and managers to strive for cultures facilitating quality improvement. The literature shows that the balance between public accountability and professional accountability has been tested within schools, colleges and universities. Whilst the best possible outcomes for learners and other stakeholders is held at the heart of the education system, the new agendas of multi-agency intervention in schools and moves towards greater personalization will offer new challenges to quality assurance and improvement. These initiatives, and others yet to come, represent important research challenges in this important field.

In this section of the text we have discussed something of the history and processes associated with the concepts of quality and accountability in education. We have noted that for some the development of quality and accountability regimes has been the decisive proof that education has entered an era of performativity where schools, colleges and universities have been bent to the will of the state. For others, although there may be technical problems with the implementation of quality and accountability processes, the quality movement has been a welcome method of levering up standards in education. In the next section of this text we go on to examine some of the key themes associated with this topic.

Part II

Themes in quality and accountability

4 Managing staff and resources for quality education

Introduction

This chapter focuses on the leadership and management of staff and resources in educational organizations following the move to more local management of schools and colleges. In doing so it explores aspects of institutional effectiveness and improvement and how the deployment and management of staff and resources is related to enhancing quality. A central tenet of this field pertains to the strong likelihood of a relationship between school resources and student outcomes since schools, colleges and universities have many groups of stakeholders and different groups may hold differing perceptions about the meaning of 'quality education'. For example, parents may be more concerned with examination results, whereas funding bodies are also likely to be concerned about value for money and the effectiveness and efficiency of financial management systems. Multiple agendas need to be met if enhanced quality and improvement are to be achieved. Internal quality assurance mechanisms need to be fit for purpose so as to support improvement as well as to withstand external quality audit and inspection. This tension between leadership actions to foster improvement and leadership actions to ensure accountability is a theme that reoccurs in this text. The field is vast, so the chapter attempts to focus on some important and contemporary issues in staff and resource management in educational organizations. To this end, the chapter explores:

- leading and managing staff and resources;
- managing professional development in schools;
- managing succession and retention in schools;
- managing staff and resources in further education;
- managing staff and resources in higher education.

The chapter concludes by emphasizing the key importance for quality improvement of the ways in which staff and resources are managed, and we note the need for further action by researchers, policy-makers and practitioners.

Leading and managing staff and resources

Although it is notoriously difficult to research empirically, evidence of a linkage between school effectiveness and staff and resources can to be found in the literature. For example, in the UK, Levačić and Vignoles (2002) have detected effects and sought to improve research in this area by advocating the need for high-quality data sets. More recently, in the US, a study by Bodine *et al.* (2008) has reported that students attending charter schools in some contexts may achieve less when compared to students attending regular public schools and that this difference may be linked to resource shortfalls in some charter schools. These authors report that some charter schools serving predominantly black students engage less experienced and less qualified teachers; reportedly school working conditions and efficacy are less favourable in these contexts when compared with those in predominantly white charter schools. Leadership and management actions in this area are also influenced by immediate contextual factors pertaining to individual organizations and may include such matters as parental, employer and community expectations and a wide range of other issues including the size and type of the institution and its geographical and social location.

Thomas and Martin (1996), Preedy *et al.* (1997), Law and Glover (2000), Coleman and Earley (2005) and Busher (2006) all offer further insights into the size and complexity of the literature in this field. These and many other authors explore facets of staff and resource management such as teamwork, staff appraisal and budgeting in both the commercial and educational sectors. Oldroyd (2005) describes human resource management (HRM) as sitting easily with contemporary notions of value for money, quality assurance and accountability and characterizes two distinct dimensions of HRM which he terms 'hard' HRM and 'soft' HRM. Hard HRM displays a strong leaning towards managerialism, with a tendency to see people as resources to be deployed and managed in the same way as material resources. Oldroyd indicates that leaders and managers subscribing to hard HRM approaches would tend to emphasize as key aspects of their work managing staff performance in order to reach targets and standards, and managing staff development and succession in pursuit of the organization's strategy. Conversely, soft HRM approaches are more people-centred and concerned with the empowerment and development of staff. Oldroyd (2005) depicts soft HRM in terms of leadership and management that enables staff to develop greater personal efficacy, individual professional efficacy and engagement with collegial professional efficacy. Individual professional efficacy is described as being concerned with the development of motivation, morale and job satisfaction to underpin individual well-being, commitment and performance. Collegial professional efficacy is linked to the creation and maintenance of a positive organizational culture in which teaching, learning and improvement can take place. The creation of open communication between colleagues, teamwork, professional learning, networking, and learning communities can all foster such a positive culture. Chapter 3 of this text has already indicated that leaders and managers in schools have a role to play in the development of both structural and cultural mechanisms that enable collegial professional efficacy. It is easier to achieve an appropriate working balance between hard and soft HRM approaches if those responsible for HRM in organizations are adequately trained and prepared for this role, so that staff commitment is fully developed and maintained. For this reason Hargreaves and Fink suggest that sustainable leadership develops rather than depletes material and human resources and that it is 'prudent and resourceful leadership that wastes neither its money nor its people' (Hargreaves and Fink, 2006: 191).

The literature also reveals strong evidence of a linkage between leadership and organizational performance (Hallinger and Heck, 1996; Frearson, 2002). To ensure that school leadership and management teams adequately link teacher professional development to the achievement of school objectives and raised performance, a system of performance management came into statutory force in September 2000 for schools in England. The performance management framework introduced in England (DfEE, 2000a, 2000b) led teachers to expect a focus upon the improvement of their knowledge and skills and also offered financial reward for those deemed to be performing well. In short, performance management is meant to identify teacher strengths and weaknesses with respect to set performance targets, so that their development needs are identified and met. For some, performance management is viewed as an important component in raising professional standards but for others it is viewed as government intervention, aimed simply at obtaining high levels of efficiency, effectiveness and accountability (Down *et al.*, 1999; Gleeson and Husbands, 2001). However, many authors have raised doubts about the management of teacher performance in this way. For example, Silcock (2002) points out that changed teaching practices take time to develop, requiring reflection on experience rather than being amenable to rapid change through performance management mechanisms. Silcock suggests that feedback on performance management from schools in England has revealed that the emotional climate of an organization is important in effecting improvement. Highly motivated staff are likely to drive up performance but many of the approaches of current performance management simply bring about 'performing for the management'. Undoubtedly, there is a link between staff relationships based upon mutual respect, collaboration and consultation and which involves a 'feel-good' factor, and the high levels of intrinsic motivation leading to the use of initiative and a desire on the part of staff to achieve high-quality work. Where performance management is a 'bolt-on' activity, it has little impact upon learner progress, the performance of staff or the overall achievement of the organization.

Moreover, Gleeson and Husbands (2003) argue that there is a growing awareness amongst researchers and practitioners that improving the quality of teaching and learning through performance management in England is not working. Advocates would suggest that performance management is rooted in local contexts and helps to provide professional learning that directly meets agreed objectives particular to the improvement journey of individual schools. However, critics like Gleeson and Husbands point to the overt and negative managerialism that is inherent in tying performance management to government targets that are not connected with the true contextual realities of teaching and learning in classrooms. Walsh (2006) contends that the influence of managerialism on the quality of education created an obsessive focus on 'measurable' outcomes and has therefore led to a narrowing of educational visions. One example suggesting that a managerialist approach to staff performance is a failure is offered by Dymoke and Harrison (2006), who provide evidence that where the professional development of the beginning teacher is rooted in performance-led school managerial systems, then a lack of support for the teacher's own career aspirations and personal and professional targets may follow.

Consistent with notions of 'hard' HRM, performance management arrangements in some schools may invite leaders and managers to highlight teacher performance deemed to be weak and in some instances lead to interventions to remediate perceived poor performance. In the UK, a distinction is drawn between performance management procedures and national capability procedures, which can lead to teacher dismissal. For instance we may cite the following quotation from the Department for Education and Employment:

> Good management with clear expectations and appropriate support will go a long way towards identifying and handling weaknesses in performance. Performance review does not form part of disciplinary or dismissal procedures. Capability procedures are already the subject of a national agreement. However, where information from the review, taken with other material, gives rise to concern about the capability of a teacher, it may lead to a decision to investigate and record performance more intensively. Where a decision is taken to enter into a formal capability procedure, the procedure supersedes performance management arrangements.
>
> (DfEE, 2000a: 17)

Although it is unlikely that teachers will perform poorly in all aspects of their work, Rhodes and Beneicke (2003) suggest that poor performance may engage a range of factors including school performance criteria; complaints from parents, pupils and teaching colleagues; monitoring by head, senior leader or middle leader; feedback from school inspectors; and poor examination results. Similarly, a study of failing teachers in the UK undertaken by Wragg *et al.* (2000) showed that chairs of governors and heads identified as indicative of unsatisfactory performance characteristics such as: poor discipline; lack of preparation or planning; problems with pupils' progress; poor personal relationships with children; low expectations of pupils; and an inability to respond to change. Rhodes and Beneicke (2003) conclude that in seeking to address issues of poor teacher performance by engaging professional development interventions, school leaders and managers need to be prepared to embrace the causes of poor performance. These causes may reside in one or more locations pertaining to the individual teacher, the post, the team, the organization or within the leadership and management of the organization itself. A balance between legitimate requirements for appropriate performance and support to facilitate improvement is advocated with benefits for the teacher concerned and, importantly, for those learners residing within their care.

The growing trend in many countries towards the decentralization of school funding has impacted on leaders and managers via increased decision-making autonomy with respect to staff and resource management and also increased accountability for the use of these funds (Coleman and Earley, 2005). However, as yet, there is little empirical evidence to suggest that decentralization has been effective in raising standards and attainment in schools and causal links are hard to establish (Levačić, 2002). The relationship between decentralization and improvement may be especially hard to establish where devolved resources are limited and hence allow little possibility for the management of these additional resources in any substantial improvement efforts. Where a larger level of funding is diverted, its good usage resides within the skill sets of those leaders and managers responsible for its effective, efficient and equitable use in quality and improvement initiatives. More resources do not necessarily mean better learner outcomes. Empirical evidence that there is indeed a direct link between more resources, smaller class sizes and enhanced results is not yet certain (Levačić and Vignoles, 2002). According to De Grauwe (2005), in some developing countries there are concerns about the possible detrimental effects of school-based management on school quality, equity between schools, the relationship between the principal and the staff, and financial transparency. In examining the advantages and disadvantages of school-based management, to ensure positive impact on school quality, overall, the necessary basic resources need to be allied to an effective school-support system. School leaders will also need regular information on school performance and advice on how they might improve and it is vital that they emphasize the motivational element in the work of the school principal.

Levačić (1997) conceptualizes educational organizations as input-process-output systems so that inputs, such as resources from the external environment, can be processed to achieve learning within the organization and provide outputs in terms of learner achievements. It is clear that some learner outputs, such as examination results, are more easily measurable than others. It is also clear in many systems that measurable academic outputs are favoured by external evaluation regimes; it is these that find their way into the public domain most easily via reports and league tables of performance. Such league tables are prevalent in all sectors of education and strongly link to market accountability, as highlighted in Chapter 2. The perception of 'good quality' will vary among individuals in the market place, hence in some countries the notion has emerged of accommodating choice through resourcing different kinds of educational organization, and allowing the management of resources to reflect different specialisms and foci. The relationship between resources and educational objectives has been explored by Sutton (1997) who points to the role of budgets and budgetary process in such linkage. Sutton argues that financial allocation to objectives may be subject to the prevailing cultural conditions (see Chapter 3) within an organization as expressed in terms of bureaucracy, power divisions, micro-politics and the degree of collegiality. In pursuing the link between resources and improvement efforts, Rhodes (2001) suggests that placing value for money at the centre of resource management in educational organizations is one way of requiring those organizations to reflect upon the robustness of financial procedures and the linkage of spending to educational priorities such as improvement. Leaders must also examine the extent to which resource management results in economy, efficiency and effectiveness. In addition, leaders must have at the forefront of their minds the extent to which resource management provides best value and equity for all learners. In order to accomplish this multifaceted and complex role leaders will, of course, also need to monitor and evaluate the spending decisions for which they are responsible.

Given that human resources are essential in school improvement journeys, there has been considerable interest in the professional development of staff and professional development has become a major resource spend in schools as well as in other sectors of education both in the UK and internationally.

Managing professional development in schools

For many teachers in the UK, professional development commences with initial teacher training and continues into the 'newly qualified teacher' induction year. Teachers are then able to engage with professional development activities, perhaps by necessity or perhaps by choice, throughout their career. Professional development is regarded as an essential component in maintaining and advancing individual personal and professional abilities, including leadership skills (Friedman and Phillips, 2001; Rhodes *et al.*, 2004a, 2004b). A national strategy for continuing professional development in the UK emerged some years ago (DfES, 2001a). The strategy promised to increase opportunities for teachers to experience relevant, focused, effective professional development, and to place professional development at the heart of school improvement. The idea that teachers can learn best 'from and with' one another was central to this strategy and this tenet is still prevalent today. Learning opportunities generated through observation, coaching, mentoring, networking and the creation of learning communities were, and still are, much favoured. Notions of effective professional development activities are likely to be first and foremost, those which enhance outcomes for learners and which also help to bring about positive change in the practice of teachers and add to the organization's overall capacity to develop, change and improve (Earley and Bubb, 2004). Leaders are able to influence both structural and cultural changes with their schools; such changes can promote staff collaboration and commitment to their own development as a means to help raise quality and improve the outcomes of learners in their charge. In Chapter 5, the notion of leadership for learning is analysed. Such leadership can occur at all levels in the school and promotes a focus on teaching and learning. Teaching staff are included in the whole organizational learning so that they may better serve the needs of all learners and promote improved outcomes.

However, demonstrating the impact of teacher professional learning is both complex and problematical (Burchell *et al.*, 2002; Davies and Preston, 2002). If the ultimate aim of teacher professional learning is to impact positively upon student learning (see Day, 1999; Bolam, 2000; Rhodes and Houghton-Hill, 2000), then barriers to the transfer of teacher learning to student learning may need to be overcome in some schools. School leaders and managers have themselves been implicated in the creation of such barriers (Adelman and Panton Walking-Eagle, 1997; Rhodes and Houghton-Hill, 2000; Peters, 2002). In Europe and internationally, professional development is widely seen as having the potential to impact positively upon teaching and learning, and hence school improvement. For example, Karagiorgi and Symeou (2006) review current in-service teacher professional development in Cyprus. They conclude that reform of the current training scheme is needed as a result of a growing gap between emerging challenges and current practices. These authors call for a decentralization of training funds and provision to be accompanied by accountability measures and quality assurance standards. They also recommend that in-service evaluation mechanisms should be established to maximize effectiveness through links to school improvement.

Kinder *et al.* (1991) have created a typology of professional learning outcomes which can have an impact on teachers at an individual, personal or professional level. These enable potential transfer at an institutional or a classroom level, which includes such issues as material and information outcomes; affective outcomes; motivational and attitudinal outcomes; knowledge and skills; institutional outcomes; and impact on practice. Moreover, teachers acquire professional knowledge in a variety of different ways. For example, teachers may find that they acquire professional knowledge by attending courses, or they may generate knowledge through reflection on their own experience of teaching. Alternatively, they may acquire knowledge through collaboration with other teachers either from the same or from another institution. Sugrue (2002) draws on the work of Cochran-Smith and Lytle (1999) to suggest three broad conceptualizations as points on a continuum emerging from the continuing professional development literature: first, there is knowledge *for* practice, where teachers engage with instruction and secure 'best practices' generated by researchers or other practitioners which can then be applied to their own practice. This broadly equates to attendance at courses. Second, there is knowledge *in* practice, where teachers themselves generate 'best practices' and modify their own practices accordingly. This implies reflective practice on the part of teachers either individually or as part of a group. Third, and finally, Sugrue suggests that there is knowledge *of* practice, where teachers are active in their own learning and are engaged in enquiry and the construction of new insights through collaborative learning in groups and networks. This implies that the parent organization is able to sustain the characteristics of a learning community. Kennedy (2005) also draws upon a similar continuum ranging from knowledge transmission to professional autonomy to locate emerging models of continuing professional development from the international professional development literature. Nine models are identified and they are classified in relation to their capacity to support professional autonomy and transformative practice. Usefully, the article explores the circumstances in which the various models could be adopted. A longitudinal study to establish the characteristics of effective teacher professional development (Boyle *et al.*, 2005) helps to relate professional development to subsequent changes in teaching practice. In this sense, the study is helping to bridge the possible gap between teacher professional learning and positive changes in the classroom experience of students. Determining if changes in practice have translated into positive effects on student attainment represents the next logical goal of this work.

Although a small number of teachers may be negative about collaborating with others (Johnson, 2003), many studies have shown that collaboration, group work and networking produce enhanced teacher learning (Rowe and Sykes, 1989; Beatty, 2000; Day *et al.*, 2002). As elaborated in Chapter 3, the establishment of a culture in which networking between colleagues enables mutual support is an important function of leadership in schools (see Bredeson and Johansson, 2000; Rhodes *et al.*, 2004b). In this context, the distribution of leadership has been seen as a potentially potent developmental experience for classroom teachers, middle leaders and senior leaders themselves (Gronn, 2000, 2003a, 2003b; Wallace, 2002; Harris, 2003, 2004; Muijs and Harris, 2003). It has also been suggested that involving teachers in identifying their own needs and in planning the professional learning experiences with which they engage is more likely to lead to their needs being met (Robinson and Sebba, 2005). A recent report has identified a place for professional development programmes that focus on the leadership skills, knowledge and understanding of deputy and assistant heads (Harris *et al.*, 2003). There is now a growing international focus upon leadership development as an important component of school improvement (Bush, 2008). It is important that leaders learn to do their jobs well for the benefit of all school stakeholders. Details of the relationship between leadership and learning will vary widely depending on national policy and local school contexts, however in a recent UK study Day *et al.* (2007) were able to closely link leadership quality with improvement and advocated the importance of leadership that fosters the learning of both staff and students.

Managing succession and retention in schools

A survey undertaken for the General Teaching Council in England in 2002 (GTCE, 2002) showed the extent of falling morale within the profession and its likely impact upon respondents' intentions to remain within the education service. The survey revealed that one in three teachers was not expecting to be teaching in five years' time. Studies dealing with exit from the profession have indicated that the seeds of non-retention may be sown at a very early career stage. For example, in a study of students who had been recruited to primary initial teacher training courses Thornton *et al.* (2002) discovered that students held deep concerns about their subsequent pay, workload, media image, status, hours and stress levels. Although subject to changing national and international economic circumstances and work availability which may present teaching as a secure occupation, in the early part of the twenty-first century the schools service in the UK has been generally ill-served by poor teacher recruitment and poor subsequent retention (DfEE, 2000c; DfES, 2001b; Dean, 2001; GTCE, 2002). The linkage between teacher retention and professional development has received considerable attention. Dean (2001) has suggested that premature loss of experienced teachers may be curtailed through professional development activities allowing for personal refreshment; Rowe and Sykes (1989) have found that professional development has yielded strong positive effects on teachers' professional self-perceptions, energy and job satisfaction. Also considering teacher self-perception, Beatty (2000) has shown that professional learning can catalyse professional growth and Day *et al.* (2002) suggest that dialogue with other teachers can help build motivation and commitment to the profession. Given that teacher development through collaboration and mutual support offers the potential to raise teacher confidence and facilitate professional learning (Rhodes and Beneicke, 2002; Rhodes *et al.*, 2004b), leadership teams need to consider how productive collaboration can be engendered within their own organizations so as to foster increased trust, commitment and retention. These aims are entirely consistent with notions of professional learning within learning communities already raised in this text. Indeed, Earley *et al.* (2002) have recommended that leadership development programmes should include a component on managing the professional development of others.

The Department for Education and Skills in the UK has completed a recent remodelling of the teaching workforce in all 23,000 schools in England and Wales (DfES, 2003a). At the heart of this remodelling is the intention to provide a better work–life balance and increase teacher job satisfaction, commitment and retention. The deployment of more support staff in schools with extended roles has been seen as an essential element in helping to reduce teacher workload. The need for deeper engagement of support staff in assessing and reporting, as well as in lesson planning, preparation and delivery has been recognized as important in remodelling the workforce (see DfES, 2003a). Boundaries that have previously defined and limited the work of support staff have weakened (Butt and Lance, 2005) and it has been increasingly understood that learning support assistants have an important role to play in supporting teachers as well as pupils (Mistry *et al.*, 2004). It is becoming evident that support staff should be enabled to develop a sense of professionalism, career structure and recognition as they become more involved in classroom teaching (Garner, 2002; Hammett and Burton, 2005). The input from support staff can improve the quality of education experienced by some learners, for example, it has been shown that learning mentors can do much to engage and include students at the margins of learning and much improve their chances of success (Rhodes, 2006).

Acute recruitment and retention problems for leadership posts, and for headship posts in particular, are experienced in the UK (see Hartle and Thomas, 2004; Howson, 2007; NCSL, 2006a, 2006b, 2007; Rhodes and Brundrett, 2009) and also internationally (see Cranston, 2007; Rhodes *et al.*, 2008), exacerbated by a demographic retirement bulge and feelings of disenchantment with leadership associated with high levels of bureaucracy, central intervention, accountability and poor work–life balance (see Draper and McMichael, 2003; Kruger *et al.*, 2005; Hargreaves and Fink, 2006; Rhodes and Brundrett, 2006; Rhodes and Brundrett, 2009). Fink and Brayman (2006) report on the increasing evidence of a potential leadership crisis in many Western countries, with the potential to undermine their school improvement initiatives. MacBeath (2006) describes an emerging leadership recruitment crisis based on teacher recruitment shortages in the Netherlands, Sweden, France and parts of Germany, but points to a lack of leadership shortages in many Asia-Pacific countries, especially in those with a good sense of leadership succession planning. As already elaborated in this text, the strong association of good quality leadership with school effectiveness and improvement is well-established. For example, Hallinger and Snidvongs (2005) refer to a large body of research conducted over the past 20 years showing that school-level leadership makes a difference to school climate and the outcomes of schooling. Leadership shortages and a dwindling talent pool from which new successors may be drawn may, therefore, have negative consequences for improvement and the enhancement of learner outcomes in a variety of schools and other educational organizations.

Pro-activity in the development of leadership successors, so that the right person is available for the right job at the right time, requires leadership talent to be recognized in others. An assessment of an individual's leadership potential is needed if human resource capable of helping to improve school quality is not to be overlooked and perhaps lost. Leadership talent identification in the UK has traditionally relied on the judgement of incumbent leaders in schools, perhaps supported by local authority consultants, and has assumed that heads and others are experienced and skilled in this respect. Identification of the characteristics of leadership talent remains an area requiring much further research (Rhodes *et al.*, 2008) with some researchers pointing to a growing empirical base indicating that an individual's set of personal and professional attributes and traits are likely precursors of leadership and leadership success (Zaccaro *et al.*, 2004; Zaccaro, 2007). In commercial organizations the identification of leadership talent and its development commonly involves the organization taking a longer-term view so that systematic preparation to address future leadership requirements can be undertaken. Much commercial sector literature emphasizes that a *laissez faire* attitude in the search for future leadership talent is irresponsible; individual performance, motivation and retention are seen as important outcomes of such active succession planning and good succession management is thought essential for the longer-term survival of the organization (Wolfe, 1996; McCall, 1998; Hirsch, 2000; Byham *et al.*, 2003; Berger and Berger, 2004; Rothwell, 2005). Given leadership shortages, securing appointments from external sources has much value; however, the growth of in-house talent pools coupled with active succession planning to create a better flow of leadership successors, now requires much more attention within schools.

Bush (2008) reviews the literature pertaining to leadership development and points to the need to match leadership learning experiences to different career stages and different work contexts, so that coherence is achieved. He suggests that the most successful leadership learning experiences occur when work-based learning is included in the overall learning experience. Lambert (2003) has argued that good school support for adult learning and talent development may enable teachers to emerge as leaders early in their careers and Stoll and Temperley (2009) have suggested that leadership development should be linked to career planning responsive to contemporary challenges. Building leadership strength at all levels in schools has been linked with leadership distribution (see Hargreaves and Fink, 2006). However, this is by no means the only leadership development mechanism available; mentoring, coaching, school projects, job rotation, shadowing, internship, peer support and networking have also been identified as valuable learning opportunities (Bush and Glover, 2004). More recently, Rhodes and Brundrett (2008, 2009) showed that good role-modelling by incumbent leaders, teamwork, trust, confidence-building, availability of advice, a commitment to professional learning and the support of leadership for this learning are all important in encouraging potential leadership successors to emerge within schools. National programmes to build leadership talent in schools have emerged in many countries. For example, in England, Scotland, France, Malta and the US leadership learning programmes and national mandatory qualifications for school headship have been adopted (see Brundrett and Crawford, 2008; Bush, 2008). It remains an area for further investigation how leadership talent identified, developed and appointed in one school context can be successfully enabled to transfer and perform well in other different school contexts (see MacBeath, 2006).

Managing staff and resources in further education

As in the schools sector, the management of staff and resources to enhance learner outcomes has been viewed as important within the college sector. An early model of 'continuous' improvement in the further education sector was provided by the Further Education Unit (1997). This model was centred on a college mission statement, needs analysis, strategic and operational plan, against a backdrop of the generation of a culture of improvement and the establishment of a quality infrastructure. Belfield and Thomas (2000) used data from further education colleges in England to examine the relationship between levels of resources and organizational performance. However, as in the schools sector, a direct link between resources and performance has been difficult to demonstrate. They conclude that explaining the link between resources and outcomes remains an important task for educational researchers.

As a means of raising standards and attainment within the sector, new legislation emerged in 2001 in the form of Statutory Instrument No. 1209. This determined that all new lecturers in further education from September of that year should have a further education teacher's qualification. This new legislation also specified that those already in post should be encouraged to gain a teaching qualification. The qualifications were based upon the standards provided by the Further Education National Training Organisation (FENTO). FENTO standards were agreed in 2001 (FENTO, 2001) and were to be used for designing accredited awards for further education teachers; to inform professional development; and to assist in appraisal and identification of training needs. The Learning and Skills Council (LSC), the government organization presently most directly involved in the funding and development of the further education sector requires all colleges to consider staff development plans on an annual basis. Inspection by Ofsted and ALI (Adult Learning Inspectorate) provided frameworks for the external evaluation of the work of further education colleges (see Chapter 8), and colleges were required to engage in post-inspection planning to address any shortfalls in performance. Staff development to provide opportunities to improve performance became more prevalent within the sector. Continuing staff development in further education has been further spotlighted by legislation requiring all teachers to experience at least 30 hours' professional development per year. It has previously been suggested that the pace of change itself within the sector creates barriers to improvement and lecturers engaged in many new developments may not have time to consolidate and develop their own knowledge and skills in a systematic way (see Martinez, 1999). The establishment of the Centre for Excellence in Leadership (CEL), mirroring the establishment of the National College for School Leadership (NCSL) for schools, indicates that leader and leadership development are increasingly being seen as key to developing the effectiveness of further education colleges across different areas of provision. However, research on the relationship between leadership and organizational performance in this sector lags behind that of the schools sector. Martinez (2002) has suggested that pro-active leadership drives the improvement of teaching and learning and that in turn has a positive effect on student retention and achievement. More recently, Muijs *et al.* (2006) have considered leader and leadership development in relation to improving and established effective providers within this sector.

They conclude that there is a likely utility of leadership development in influencing the effectiveness of individual organizations. Although many of the basic tenets pertaining to the management of staff and resources established in schools are likely to transfer to other educational organizations, there is still much research to be undertaken concerning the contextualization of these tenets within the further education sector.

Managing staff and resources in higher education

In many countries of the world, the desire to maintain and improve quality of teaching and research in higher education is increasingly driven by the need to respond to the demands of market accountability. The emergence of public reporting on quality and national and international league tables has served to focus greater attention on the strategic and operational use of staffing and resources to ensure both good reputation and freer access to streams of students and other funding. Although higher education in the UK possesses a history of research capability, academic staff autonomy and high levels of self-management, many of the basic tenets of staff and resource management highlighted in the schools sector are likely also to apply and translate into the higher education sector. The impacts of managerialism and performativity, frequently mentioned within the schools sector, are becoming increasingly evident in higher education (see Chapter 3). In the UK, Hopfl (2000) argues that the expansion of higher education over the past decade and a half has brought greater pressures on staff and students alike. Some of the negative impacts upon staff are portrayed as stemming from an overemphasis on performance, the personal costs of excessive and competing demands and the increasing bureaucracy. Managerial threat to personal autonomy is also highlighted in a study of two business schools in two statutory universities in the UK (Hoecht, 2006). This study explores academics' perception of the impact of quality assurance on their professional autonomy. Most of the interviewees thought that there were benefits for students; however, current systems were seen as overly bureaucratic and required large amounts of documentation and box-ticking and were therefore overladen with opportunity costs. The study concludes that quality management is now an integral part of university life and that higher levels of accountability can be accommodated if quality audits are tailored to promote learning and innovation rather than bureaucratic control. Morley (2003) cautions that quality control in UK higher education presents the danger that academics and managers are now valued for their contribution to perceived organizational performance, perhaps at the expense of their subject or professional knowledge. In another work, this author also contends that quality audit is a potent force of surveillance and normalization and its introduction has reduced and regulated academic staff autonomy while purporting to extend the entitlements of other stakeholders (Morley, 2005). It has been suggested that increased external accountability measures and competition in higher education have led to more distrust and separation between management and staff (Prichard, 2000).

In the US the notion of student engagement, as expressed in their development and learning, has emerged as an important concept in the research literature on quality in higher education. This has been seen by some to be helpful in advancing, defining and evaluating academic quality and offers a route to information needed to satisfy accountability demands. For example student engagement, expressed in terms of student involvement, faculty–student interaction and student academic and social integration, has been linked to notions of student learning, development and retention and J. F. Ryan (2005) suggests that a closer examination of institutional expenditure and student engagement is timely. In the UK, a study by Rhodes and Nevill (2004) showed that common student concerns about teaching and learning, finances, workload and support could be managed within the institution and enhance the likelihood that students could achieve better integration and be retained. Consultation with students about their experience of teaching and learning, and how it can be improved, has become increasingly commonplace in universities (see Campbell and Li, 2008; Gaspar *et al.*, 2008; Ozolins *et al.*, 2008). Widening participation and other changes in the higher education student body, reflecting increasing numbers of part-time, distant and mature students with differing learning needs, has led many institutions to place greater reliance upon information and communications technology (ICT) as a convenient means of communication and instruction. Although cost-efficiency may be an outcome of instruction via ICT, questions emerge with respect to the quality and effectiveness of teaching and learning mediated via developing computer-based learning environments. For example, Kirkwood and Price (2005) conclude that although ICT can enable new forms of teaching and learning to take place, it cannot ensure that effective and appropriate learning outcomes are achieved. The new opportunities presented by virtual learning environments need to be balanced against sound pedagogy and learning opportunities that will foster more active and engaged learners. Despite such advances there is still much research pertaining to staff and resource management to be undertaken within this sector and the impact of centrally and institutionally driven quality agendas remains to be determined.

Conclusion

A key focus of this chapter has been to consider the leadership and management of staff and resources, so that quality may be improved and learner outcomes may be enhanced. The assumption that the devolution of greater funding and responsibility to schools would lead to such improvement is hard to show empirically. The management of staff and resources across schools, further education colleges and higher education institutions is a vast field to explore and the chapter has sought to draw out important points of focus, many of which translate across all three sectors, each with its own attached collection of popular and politically driven expectations and subject to the stakeholders they serve and the national policy contexts in which they function. Despite these contextual differences, and differences in what might be perceived as a 'quality education', educational organizations within these sectors hold commonalities in the shared understandings of the purposes of education and a desire to express this in the quality of their provision and the realization of the visions of their learners. The performance of staff is clearly an important element in achieving these aims and the chapter explored facets of the 'hard' and 'soft' approaches to staff management. Within all sectors, an increasing prevalence of managerialism is detectable. This has been hailed by advocates as a true road to achieving high-quality and improved outcomes, and by critics as a certain route to staff demoralization and de-professionalization and the risk of exit from the profession and falling standards.

'Soft' human resource management displays a more people-centred approach to improvement and quality improvement. In the schools sector particularly, this softer approach has been characterized through efforts to develop collaboration, trust, networking and professional development and learning. However, in all sectors, leadership and management have been demonstrated to have a role to play in addressing performance through efforts to engage staff commitment, motivation and a sense of shared vision with learners in mind. Indeed, leadership for professional learning, staff and support deployment, succession management and effective pedagogy cross sectors and international boundaries and link to the improvement journeys of all educational organizations. Overall, the management of staff and resources is fundamental to outcomes, and quality and self-evaluating organizations will no doubt be anxious to ensure that details of material and financial resource management do lead to the satisfaction of stakeholder demands and best possible learner outcomes, as well as satisfying external evaluators and auditors who have potent influence upon the internal and external perceptions of the organization. Although the knowledge base is still expanding and much research remains to be done, as indicated throughout this chapter, the field is of key importance in quality improvement and acts as an important basis for researcher, policy-maker and practitioner improvement action.

5 Leadership for high-quality teaching and learning

Introduction

The development of site-based management in education created a strong impetus for research into the management of educational organizations in areas such as human resources and finance since these topics had previously been unfamiliar to professional educators. Not surprisingly, the challenges presented by such new and extended areas of responsibility evoked concern amongst leaders and managers about the capabilities required in accounting for these issues perhaps, in some cases, at the expense of a full focus on the teaching and learning already established in their organizations. These new demands impacted most upon leaders and managers in schools following decentralization, and in colleges following incorporation. However, the possibility of a preoccupation with resource management at the expense of a full focus on teaching, learning and student outcomes has also been detected in higher education. For example, Johnson and Deem (2003) suggest that at institutional and individual levels some manager-academics may have shifted their focus to the organizational and resource implications of the student body as a whole, perhaps to the detriment of their understanding of student concerns.

However, the quality of teaching in schools and colleges has long been associated with the likelihood of successful student outcomes and research shows that quality of teaching is the single most important factor in successful education (Barber, 1997). For this reason recent developments in the field of educational leadership and management have re-emphasized that leadership must focus on educational outcomes, and that leadership for learning is central to enhancing the quality of schooling. Thus, there is no more important area of accountability in education than teaching and learning. In this chapter we examine:

- ways in which instructional leadership can set an agenda for leadership actions;
- links between leadership and learning;
- the influence and impact of learning-centred leadership;
- the lasting influence of the idea of learning communities;
- recent interest in personalized learning;
- the growing importance of student voice.

We conclude by suggesting that new approaches to accountability need to be sought to enable the further promotion of learning-focused educational organizations.

Instructional leadership

During the 1980s a growing body of research on effective schools, both in the US and internationally, focused the attention of policy-makers and scholars on the importance of leadership by the principals of educational institutions (see, for instance, Bossert *et al.*, 1982; Purkey and Smith, 1983). Meanwhile, efforts to study the impact of principal leadership had begun to identify the professional leadership dimensions of the principal's role that impacted school success (for example, Erickson, 1967; Gross and Herriott, 1965). Overall, this research asserted that the 'instructional leadership' role of the principal was crucial to school effectiveness (Bossert *et al.*, 1983; Leithwood and Montgomery, 1982). Nonetheless, as noted by Hallinger (2010: 122), even at the height of the effective schools movement, advocacy for principals to exercise 'strong instructional leadership' was subject to a critique which questioned the underlying assumptions of instructional leadership by principals and its viability as a dominant paradigm for conceptualizing school leadership (for example, Barth, 1986; Cuban, 1988). This trend increased during the 1990s, as scholars interested in school improvement argued the case for transformational leadership (Leithwood, 1994) and teacher leadership (Barth, 1990, 2001) as alternative conceptualizations. However, the rise of the accountability movement led, once again, to a focus on school leadership in general and instructional leadership in particular (see, for instance, Gewertz, 2003; Hallinger, 2010).

In its current form, instructional leadership embraces leadership actions that develop institutional culture to enhance both teacher and student learning (Sheppard, 1996; Spillane, 2004). Instructional leaders talk to teachers about teaching, encourage collaboration between teachers, empower teachers to make decisions, and encourage professional growth, teacher leadership, autonomy and self-efficacy (Blase and Blase, 2004). Successful instructional leaders are able to encourage those conditions that can constitute a professional learning community of students and teachers.

In the UK, it has been noted that a focus on student learning requires a commitment both to enquire into pupils' own perspectives on their learning and to use this information to inform developments in pedagogy and learning (Fielding *et al.*, 1999). Correlatively, a focus on teacher learning requires a commitment to pedagogic development and the creation of an environment where teachers are confident to become learners (Southworth, 2000). Instructional leadership is strongly connected with teaching and learning, including both student learning and the professional learning of teachers. The difference between a curriculum-centred view and associated transmission of content and a learning-centred view is explored by MacBeath *et al.* (2007), who contend that teaching to stimulate learning requires teachers to create environments supportive of learning which are mediated through their good working relationships with learners in the community and their ability to engage students through stimulating and well-communicated interaction. Thus, leaders need a strong understanding of pedagogy if student and staff processes and outcomes are to be enhanced, with concomitant implications for leaders' own professional development. There are those who argue that instructional leadership has been reincarnated as the new paradigm for twenty-first-century school leadership (Hallinger, 2010: 122). However, the concept of 'leadership for learning' has increasingly come to the forefront in research, theory development and policy-making. For this reason it is to this concept that we now turn.

The link between leadership and learning

The term 'leadership for learning' has been used increasingly to represent a re-focusing of leadership activity on the core issues of education. MacBeath and Dempster (2009) argue that there are five major principles that underpin leadership for learning: shared or distributed leadership; a focus on learning; creation of the conditions favourable for learning; creation of a dialogue about leadership and learning; and the establishment of a shared sense of accountability. It is this complex nexus of leadership functions that constitute the key to the relationship between what leaders do and the achievement of educational organizations.

Despite the increasing emphasis on leadership and learning, unpacking the ways in which leaders can impact on learning has been problematic. Theories of learning have tended traditionally to offer two opposing views, emphasizing either teacher-centred or pupil-centred approaches, which can be characterized as 'top-down' or 'bottom-up' approaches (Brundrett and Silcock, 2002). More recent work draws on developments in cognitive theory (see Shayer and Adey, 2002) in order to offer an alternative notion that attempts to resolve this dichotomy by supporting 'co-constructivist' techniques (Broadfoot, 2000) whereby twin perspectives that are both 'top down' *and* 'bottom up' are encouraged (Biggs, 1992). Such co-constructed forms of learning integrate teacher- or subject-centred systems with pupil-centred approaches into a third partnership approach (Silcock and Brundrett, 2006). Within this co-constructivist approach, all members of staff cooperate, negotiate, resolve differences, mediate between options, and act to reach decisions that will enhance student learning. It also follows that staff will work in partnership with students in order to enable them to appreciate alternatives, experiment with radical positions, and show a tolerance generally untested within mono-cultural settings (Brundrett and Silcock, 2002: 91). These new perspectives on learning theory have created the potential for a revolution in the role of school leaders at all levels, as it becomes clear that new forms of leadership emphasizing collaboration and distribution of power and authority are themselves central to learning (Burton and Brundrett, 2005). Heads in schools and principals in colleges are strongly encouraged to understand the importance of their role in enhancing the learning experience of students and are urged to ensure that support for teaching and learning is identified as a key element of their leadership responsibility and accountability. For some, the adoption of a learner-centred approach to teaching and learning has been seen as having the potential to effect better learner inclusion, engagement and hence improved achievement. The link between leadership and learning is emphasized by Leithwood *et al.* (2006) who claims that school leadership is second only to classroom teaching as an influence on pupil learning. Similarly, PricewaterhouseCoopers (2007) suggest that the behaviour of school leaders has great impact on student performance and affirm that there is widespread recognition that school leaders have a vital role in raising the quality of teaching and learning within their schools.

Becoming a 'learning-centred' institution has emerged as a term denoting that a school or college has placed both student and staff learning at the core of its work. As already mentioned in this text, staff learning represents an important means of creating increased capacity for organizational improvement. Coupled with a culture that fosters collaboration and trust, staff learning has an important role to play in serving the organization in its endeavours to change, improve and further support student learning outcomes. Links between leadership and learning may be seen in leaders' actions to enable the learning of others, including leaders themselves (Swaffield and MacBeath, 2009). For example, in some organizations, leadership for learning may be about empowering middle leaders and teachers to take a direct lead in teaching and learning (for example, see Fitzgerald and Gunter, 2006; Frost, 2008). Alternatively, understandings of leadership for learning may be characterized by senior leadership's reliance upon assessment and outcome data to reward perceived good teacher performance as expressed in a desire for improved outcomes in the US conception of 'instructional leadership' discussed earlier in this chapter (see Elmore, 2000; Blase and Blase, 2004; Spillane, 2004).

Learning-centred leadership

It has been argued with some cogency that if we are to achieve the goal of implementing leadership for learning the focus of leadership itself will need to shift to what Fink and Hargreaves have termed 'deep and broad' learning (Hargreaves and Fink, 2006). Leaders who seek to achieve this goal will attempt to create an environment in which learning is at the centre of every decision, policy, practice or custom, and they will be 'passionately, creatively, obsessively and steadfastly committed to enhancing "deep" and broad learning for all students – learning for understanding, learning for life, learning for a knowledge society' (Fink, 2005: xvii). Fink (2010) suggests seven sets of learning that help in redefining leadership: contextual knowledge; political acumen; emotional understanding; understanding learning; critical thinking; making connections; and futures thinking. This list of skills and knowledge is impressive, but if leaders are to be produced who possess these qualities then leadership development programmes will need to be created or adapted significantly.

Emphasizing the importance of learning-centred leadership and the ways in which school leaders can influence teaching and learning both in classrooms and across the whole school, Southworth (2004) offers the delineation of six levels of learning, from pupil level to learning networks level. These six levels allow us to show some examples of how leaders may act:

- *the pupil level of learning* where leaders may use outcome data to make appropriate interventions;
- *the teacher level of learning* where leaders may enable opportunities for teachers to learn from one another as a means of embedding new and improved practices;

- *the collaborative staff learning level* facilitated by the establishment of structural and cultural changes within the school;
- *the organizational learning level* where professional growth may enable a learning community to be established, characterized by trust and openness;
- *the leadership learning level* charged with the wider promotion of learning-centred leadership within the organization;
- *the learning networks level* where the engagement of a variety of empowered staff is most likely to lead to the adoption of enhanced classroom learning opportunities.

It is clear from this analysis that learning-centred leadership involves the learning of students and staff and also the learning of leaders themselves. It offers insights into leadership actions that can serve to raise quality through a focus on teaching and learning intended to raise the outcomes of learners. Hallinger and Heck (1999) suggest that learning-centred leaders may act to influence learning and teaching outcomes in three different ways. They may influence outcomes *directly* by personal intervention, *reciprocally* by working alongside other teachers or, most commonly, *indirectly* via the agency of teachers and other staff.

Through reliance on teachers and other staff as key agents in raising quality and outcomes, school leaders are likely to recognize that positive influences on teaching and learning can be sought through their influence on staff motivation, commitment and supportive working conditions. For example, helping to establish good standards of pupil behaviour, engagement in learning and the achievement of good outcomes can, in turn, serve to further motivate teachers within the school (see Leithwood *et al.*, 2006; Addison and Brundrett, 2008). Success in improving student outcomes is associated with the establishment of an achievement-focused school culture, in which care and trust are part of the expectations of the senior leadership of the school (Day *et al.*, 2007). Southworth (2004) has advocated the distribution of learning-centred leadership amongst staff to increase the focus on teaching and learning throughout the organization. Such an approach can impact positively on a teacher's decision-making capacity and therefore have the potential to impact on student learning and achievement. For this reason, middle leaders have become a key focus for research in recent years (Burton and Brundrett, 2005) since middle leaders are closer to students and can transmit strategies that enhance student achievement amongst colleagues through the creation of departmental cultures (Busher, 2006).

Learning communities

Some of the benefits of the establishment of schools and other educational organizations as learning communities were referred to in Chapter 3. Considering schools in the UK, Busher (2006) suggests that the dynamics of a learning community involve the combined voices of leaders, teachers, pupils, support staff and other adults working together to foster student learning. He suggests that a learning community may be as small as a department or as big as the whole school. Bezzina (2008) reports on the creation of a learning community in a school in Malta, where the head successfully distributed leadership and encouraged teacher leadership and decision-making in order to transmit a shared focus on team working, classroom practice and pupils' learning throughout the school. In the US, Keedy (1999) has cautioned that without the engagement of principals who value teacher leadership, there is less likelihood of teachers transforming schools into learning communities and realizing the attendant benefit of revitalizing schools for all learners. The benefits to schools and other educational organizations of developing the characteristics of a learning community are perceived to be associated with learning that enables more rapid responses to changing environments (Stoll *et al.*, 2003; Stoll and Louis, 2007), enhanced staff development (Stoll *et al.*, 2006) and the production of better outcomes (Cochran-Smith and Lytle, 1999; Roberts and Pruitt, 2003). Effective professional learning communities take collective responsibility for staff and student learning and need leadership to enable the necessary background structural and cultural support for openness, inclusion and mutual trust to develop. The development of learning communities, for many, would be incomplete without the input of learner voice leading to better understanding of learners' experience of teaching and learning with the organization and how it may be improved. This may involve changes fostering greater personalization of learning and it is to this topic that this chapter now turns.

Personalized learning

The UK government's vision for children's services, as expressed in the *Every Child Matters* agenda (DfES, 2003b), proposed a reshaping of children's services to help achieve a number of key outcomes including that children should: be healthy; stay safe; enjoy and achieve; make a positive contribution; and achieve economic well-being. The thinking behind *Every Child Matters* is not new for most schools and, as the DfES acknowledges: 'A combination of high expectations, innovative thinking and a broad view of supporting children and young people are common features of highly successful schools' (DfES, 2003b: 3). These core ideas are increasingly embedded in the work of central organizations whose work impacts on learning and teaching such as the NCSL, the TDA, and the QCA, and Ofsted. The Teaching and Learning Research Programme (TLRP), one of the largest educational research initiatives ever mounted, has undertaken a series of major research studies on the topic of personalized learning. The report of the TLRP group notes that in September 2004 the DfES produced a model which reveals that personalized learning consists of five core elements, supplemented by a range of policies and practices including: giving pupils opportunities to decide their own learning objectives; providing guidance on asking questions, giving feedback and using criteria; helping pupils assess their own and one another's learning; and giving pupils opportunities to assess one another's work (Pollard and James, 2004: 6). It has been recognized that personalized learning is increasingly creating a new agenda for curriculum leadership (see Burton and Brundrett, 2005) and Whitty and Wisby (2007) identified children's rights, active citizenship, school improvement and the greater personalization of learning as the four main drivers for the need to access pupil voice.

There is a danger that such activities can be resisted by teachers, especially when preparing children for external testing. The wish to further engage pupils in learning via enhanced personalization may be seen by some as potentially damaging to the established standards agenda in schools, which carries the attendant pressure of public reporting of academic performance to the 'market' of pupils, parents and other stakeholders. Conversely, the proponents of greater personalization point to the benefits of increased pupil inclusion, greater pupil ownership of learning and the contribution of the voices of pupils in helping to guide new perspectives on the quality in teaching and learning and hence potential outcomes. To respond to such fears, leadership actions may be aimed at improving practice in relation to personalization activities. For example, leaders could build confidence and support among staff by presenting evidence of the positive outcomes possible and showing example successes from their own school or reported from work in other schools. Leaders can also be sensitive to any anxiety experienced by pupils and teachers and ensure that other school policies and initiatives are in harmony with the principles and values that underpin pupil consultation and the emergence of pupil voices that are listened to and are heard (see Pollard and James, 2004: 13). It is important that appropriate support and accountability systems are put in place to support this approach (Pollard and James, 2004: 25) but, if followed through, a more partnership-oriented approach becomes possible that will enable more inclusive approaches to school self-evaluation that accord with recent trends in inspection regimes.

Student voice

As noted in Chapter 3, student voice has been promoted as a means to inform student integration and improve teaching and learning and retention in the higher education sector (for example, see Rhodes and Nevill, 2004; Campbell and Li, 2008). It is commonplace to find great importance attached to teaching evaluations, outcome data and staff–student consultation concerning quality issues in both the internal and external quality frameworks applied within this sector. In the UK college sector, student representation is also well-established as a contributor to quality improvement (LSC, 2006). Although there is little research in this area, the incorporation of student voice in fostering improved student pro-activity and engagement in learning is recognized as having an important role to play (Collinson, 2007). This author also identifies that the development of higher levels of student empowerment and collaboration with staff in decision-making has implications for the emergence of student leadership in this sector.

The place of pupil voice in improvement activities in schools has attracted much recent national and international attention. In the UK, Cruddas (2007) has put forward the notion of accessing pupil voice as a common sense approach if one wants to know what children want. This approach has been explored in a UK primary school, where Papatheodorou (2002) established that pupils showed much awareness about the physical limitations of their learning environment and its impact on their learning experience. The study showed that this input was able to contribute to discussion with teachers so that learning could be advanced. In a US-based study, Mitra (2005) reported that student voice initiatives aimed at including students in school decision-making can range from allowing students to voice opinions through to full collaboration with staff. Rudduck and Flutter (2000: 78) suggest that time and careful preparation are needed to build a climate in which teachers and pupils feel comfortable working together on a constructive view of teaching and learning. It has been suggested that such preparation time is needed because some teachers may consider student voice as a further threat to teacher professionalism (Fielding, 2001: 105). In a recent study, Frost and Holden (2008) established that student voices in schools have not been as prominent as the voices of adults and in an Australian study Lewis and Burman (2008) elaborate areas of decision-making, such as management issues, that teachers would not feel comfortable in negotiating with students. As Martin *et al.* (2005) suggest, in many schools adult support is needed to bring forward the voice of students so that they may play a role within their learning communities. Exploring the engagement of Greek secondary school students in discussions about teaching and learning, Mitsoni (2006) further established the importance of adult support for student voice and cautioned that such support may place considerable additional demands upon those teachers who are not part of already established learning communities.

Flutter and Rudduck (2004) draw on Hart (1997) to illustrate how leaders can seek to ascend a 'ladder' of pupil participation along a continuum ranging from exclusion from consultation, via being listened to, to becoming active participants along with adults. Given that there are large experience and power differences between adults and pupils in schools, it is not entirely surprising that MacBeath (2006a) reports that the term 'pupil voice' has generally remained a limited conception of letting young people 'have a say' within the bounds of established school constraints. Leaders in schools need to consider how, and to what extent, empowerment can be helpfully incorporated to allow the constructive involvement of pupils in decision-making and decision-questioning. As Frost *et al.* (2009) note, a shift in organizational vision may be necessary if the voices of pupils are to be taken seriously. Nevertheless, Frost (2008) contends that developing student leadership is essential if leadership is to be truly distributed in school communities. Again, leaders need to ask themselves about the feasibility, acceptability and sustainability of engaging student voice and student leadership in fostering improvements in teaching and learning and in helping to develop active pupil citizenship within their school.

Conclusion

The movement to site-based management of educational institutions created a new set of challenges for educational leaders in areas such as financial and human resource management. For this reason the chief executive role of educational leaders has been increasingly emphasized. However, recent years have witnessed a growing awareness that educational leaders must focus on learning and teaching activities if educational outcomes are to be enhanced. Put simply, educational institutions exist to promote and enable learning and educational leaders must account for the quality of the learning that takes place under their supervision. This realization is encapsulated in the emergence of terms such as 'leadership for learning' and 'learning-centred leadership' (see also Rhodes and Brundrett, 2009).

The role of leaders and the locus and ownership of leadership in relation to teaching and learning has been challenged by new and emerging conceptions in pedagogy and andragogy. For instance, in recent years there has been a notable movement towards constructivist approaches to teaching and learning in all sectors of education. The extent to which this shift in thinking is reflected in classrooms is subject to debate, but there is evidence that approaches to teaching that take account of student voice and promote learning at all levels throughout organizations are effective in enhancing learning outcomes. As part of this new landscape of learning a new architecture of leadership is also emerging, that empowers both staff and students to take control of leadership functions. This adds complexity to accountability functions, since heads and principals remain accountable for the success or failure of their organizations. Nonetheless, new approaches to accountability need to be sought to enable the further promotion of learning-focused educational organizations.

6 Educational institutions as permeable and accountable organizations

Introduction

The key focus of this chapter is accountability and its relationship with competing sets of stakeholder requirements. The title of the chapter is intended to convey the notion of the permeable boundaries of educational organizations, traversed by partnerships with stakeholders who may offer advantages to learners but may also present competing demands and differing understandings of quality in education. The management of these boundaries to secure quality and improvement benefits and minimize difficulties is an important leadership function within all educational organizations.

Senge *et al.* (1996) have highlighted this permeability as classroom learning extends into museums, businesses and homes, as teachers undertake professional learning in other organizations and as those in the wider community return to classrooms to renew their learning. Busher (2006) also refers to the semi-permeable nature of school boundaries which need to accommodate a two-way movement between internal and external stakeholders. For example, as Busher points out, schools and teachers residing within local communities hold relationships with parents and other community members which inevitably result in cross-boundary exchanges and transactions. Although members of staff, learners, parents, governors and central government are ever-present as stakeholders, partnership with other community stakeholders is likely to be influenced by contextual circumstances and opportunities presenting themselves at any particular time. A review of some of the major stakeholders with interests in the efficiency, effectiveness, equity and performance of educational organizations is offered in Chapter 7. An introduction to the nature of accountability and an exploration of the relationship between senior leaders and governors was provided in Chapter 2. We now seek to build on this introduction and explore the relationship between accountability and stakeholders in schools, colleges and in higher education.

In constructing this chapter we draw on the analysis of accountability research, developed by Webb (2005), who identifies three emergent themes pertaining to the purpose, the effects and the understanding of accountability. The first of these themes relates to intent and who holds whom accountable and for what. The second theme relates to the effects of accountability in terms of impact upon professional work and the relationship of accountability to sanction and reward. Finally, the third theme pertains to an understanding of how external pressure for accountability is made sense of and influences schools' own conceptions of accountability. For this reason this chapter examines:

- who is accountable for what in education;
- the impact on leaders of accountability in education;
- leadership and school improvement;
- educational institutions' own conceptions of accountability: developing a culture of self-review.

Since much of the discussion in these sections focuses on the specific impact of changes in accountability regimes as they apply to schools, additional sections are also provided that focus on the particularities of:

- accountability and stakeholders in further education;
- accountability and stakeholders in higher education.

We conclude by emphasizing that school leaders need to understand their role in facilitating and directing a network of relationships both inside and outside the school if they are to attain the best possible outcomes for the learners in their care.

Who is accountable for what in education?

To be accountable to stakeholders is to offer an account of performance and to justify this in relation to established or expected standards. Accountability operates when those who have been given responsibilities and decision-making power present an account of their performance for judgement concerning successes and shortcomings. In education, professionals are accountable to many stakeholders. The attendant mechanisms of data collection for accountability purposes are likely to include self-evaluation (see Chapter 8) and external inspection (see Chapter 9). Coleman and Earley (2005) describe the multiple accountabilities of the education profession in terms of the:

- hierarchies in which it is embedded;
- market;
- networks of collaboration;
- interior authority;
- ties to the profession and to the community;
- democratic values, views and preferences in response to clients.

Accountability is a generally accepted norm in democratic systems of government and it is well understood that the general public hold their elected representatives to account for their performance via periodic electoral ballots. In educational organizations, accounting to the public domain requires leaders and teachers to enable attempts to measure service outputs through internal and external evaluation and inspection measures. Depending on sector, output data is likely to include reference to examination passes and also data pertaining to attendance, stakeholder satisfaction, progression and retention. Over recent years, successive governments in the UK and in other countries have introduced market-based approaches to accountability in order to engage the voices of the recipients of educational services and assess their satisfaction or dissatisfaction with organizational performance.

Hartley (2008) suggests that the marketization of education in England began in the 1980s with the advent of national testing and the rise of competition between providers to position themselves as 'schools of choice' for parents and learners. In the US, Garn (2001) reported on the rise of charter schools with less reliance on bureaucratic regulations but greater levels of accountability based on these schools being the choice of parents and learners. In this respect, a move from bureaucratic to market accountability was noted. Newman and Jahdi (2009) suggest that the marketization of further and higher education, over a similar period, has led to an increase in marketing activities in both these sectors. Hemsley-Brown and Oplatka (2006) refer to the transfer of marketing techniques well-established in business to educational organizations seeking to gain a competitive edge nationally, and in the case of some institutions, internationally. Oplatka and Hemsley-Brown (2004) review the research literature on school marketing and suggest the need for more research into the processes and practice of marketing in schools, leading to the evolution of coherent models well contextualized in the educational field, rather than the business field. It is intended that the outcome of the competition fostered by market accountability will be expressed through patronage of successful organizations at the expense of those who are less successful. Choice between organizations, should this be available, is likely to be influenced by data based on performance placed in the public domain. This approach is also intended to offer an opportunity for less successful organizations to become more successful and demonstrate their new success through measures of account.

There seems little doubt that the effects of this market-driven approach are that more power has been given to the consumer and that central government is more concerned than ever that educational organizations should account for the money that is spent on them (Farrell and Law, 1999). This means that school leaders need to deal not only with the immediate geographical and socioeconomic environment of the school but also with a wide variety of national and local organizations. It is within the local environment that stakeholders such as parents, learners, community groups, governors, other schools, the local authority and local employers are most likely to reside. Other stakeholders, such as central government, government agencies, universities, colleges and other employers, are located more distantly but they are nevertheless potentially very influential via their power, authority and desired relationships with schools. Joyce *et al.* (1999) advocate the involvement of broader communities, including parents as well as teachers, heads and employers in bringing about school improvement. However, it has been established that achieving parental involvement is one of the most difficult areas of school improvement, especially in economically deprived areas (Muijs *et al.*, 2004). The improvement of home–school links remains a challenge for leadership in many schools, and is an important area for development given the potential advantages for learners either directly within the school or indirectly via the opinions and values learners carry with them to the school (see Chapter 7). In the UK, the Teacher Development Agency (TDA, 2006a) offered a support toolkit to enable schools to undertake stakeholder mapping as a basis for the development of support and to foster stakeholder commitment to change and improvement.

Schools are thought to be uniquely placed to promote community cohesion and accountability at neighbourhood level, and school governing bodies in the UK are now charged with many of the key decisions affecting schools (Bird, 2003). Governors are seen as representatives of the local community; ideally governing body member-ship should reflect different ethnic, cultural and faith backgrounds. The governing body sets school improvement objectives with the head, sets targets for the head's own performance and is instrumental in reviewing the head's performance and pay against these targets. They are responsible for ensuring that the school is accountable to the community it serves, a role reinforced by legislation to increase the proportion of parents serving on governing bodies through a new category of 'community' gov-ernor brought within the Education Act 2002. However, what represents quality in education to one stakeholder may not represent quality in education to another. Stewart and Walsh (1990) suggest three questions to test the creation of a framework for quality:

- Is the core service fit for the purpose for which it was designed?
- Are the physical surroundings in which the service is delivered appropriate?
- What is the service relationship between those who provide and those who receive the service?

These questions relate to a market-based approach to accountability and emphasize important elements of stakeholder interest. The answers to these questions fall within the remit of school leadership and management within decentralized systems and prompt consideration of accountability for what? and to whom?

The impact on leaders of accountability in education

Webb (2005) refers to the emergent market-based approach to accountability noted earlier as the 'new' accountability, intended to make education and the work of educa-tors more visible through inspections, observations and the public reporting of test scores. Critics of this approach have raised questions about the linkage of performance and exam scores to student achievement, and highlighted the associated risks of demoralizing and de-professionalizing teachers who may be driven to simply 'teach to the test'. Critics also point out that exam scores may be strongly influenced by differ-ences and inequalities between schools, rather than being solely related to teacher per-formance. In the UK, the local authority has traditionally played a key role in providing advice and inspection work. However, there has been a significant reduction in the capacity of local authorities to do this over recent years and quality assurance has been placed more firmly in the hands of external inspection teams contracted to bodies such as Ofsted (see Chapter 9). One of the most profound impacts of these changes is that, despite a growing self-evaluation element to inform external inspection audits (see Chapter 8), a reduction in the professional autonomy of local authorities, schools and teachers has occurred and, overall, opportunities for professional accountability have been reduced.

These changes and the problems associated with them are an international phenomenon. For instance, in the US, Ryan (2005) reports on the 'No Child Left Behind' (NCLB) Act of 2001, that holds individuals and organizations accountable through auditable performance standards. Ryan uses this as illustrative of how an audit culture is shaping educational practices and relationships. It is proposed that this legislation forces organizational reliance on performance indicators as a key mechanism for improving student achievement. Ryan adds that a lack of discussion on what educational outcomes should be is a further indication of the emergence of a climate of control. It is suggested that the NCLB accountability requirements are rooted in the market-based approach to accountability, whereby unsuccessful schools improve or close as learners seek out more successful schools. Accepting that educational accountability is a fundamental right of citizens in a democratic society, Ryan (2004, 2005) calls for more democratic approaches to accountability where schools and their communities hold themselves responsible for what they are doing and communities are involved in the setting of external and internal standards. A key facet of accountability is that it should provide information upon which improvement decisions can be made, hence the best approaches to improve student learning and outcomes can become established. To many, it is fundamental that stakeholders are engaged in working together to enable educational organizations to improve and to contribute to a shared focus on actions formulated in response to the outcomes of evaluations. As stakeholders residing within educational organizations leaders, managers and teachers in schools are generally most directly involved in making decisions about the efficient, effective and appropriate use of resources. In a democratic notion of accountability, they should, in turn, be held accountable by other stakeholders so that learner interests are best served by actions promoting the linkage of resources to shared educational objectives and ensuring that educational equity is promoted. However, it is likely to be true in schools, colleges and to some extent in higher education that whilst being held to account for actions that translate into the measurable outcomes achieved by learners, it is difficult to relate satisfactorily, even via value-added measures, the influence of the nature of their intake upon these outcomes.

Moos (2005) reports on how schools in Denmark cope with external demands for accountability made on them by different stakeholders. This author sets these demands against the need to build and sustain trust in, and trust from, staff within the school. The school leader is seen as pivotal in brokering good relations with and between external stakeholders and the school staff. The struggle between accountability and trust is explored and it is suggested that democratic leadership in many countries, including Denmark, is potentially threatened as decentralization leads to greater emphasis on economic values. Whilst some school leaders and parents favour this, others perceive that traditional trust in schools is being challenged. In a study of Danish school principals Moos reveals:

> Overall, the Danish school leaders involved in the study do not feel pressured by external control. They find that most of the means for setting goals and for

evaluation initiated by the local authorities are good tools for leading the educational processes in schools. They translate and transform the external accountability demands into internal educational tools.

(Moos, 2005: 322)

It is concluded that school leaders have an important role to play in negotiations between political demands and the experiences of professionals in schools.

In Australia, McWilliam and Perry (2006) suggest that school principals and other school leaders are under increasing pressure to enhance school image, reputation and achieve narrowly defined performance targets, at the expense of investment in a creative and risk-taking learning environment. These authors suggest that in a market-driven system of accountability, vulnerability to accusations of student failure, wastage of resources and decline of standards are likely to be damaging to autonomy, experiment and risk-taking. A fear of risk-taking is seen as potentially an important detraction from learning. In New Zealand, Court (2004) argues that ethical forms of professional collegiality and trusting relationships, which have been found to be important in the development of effective teaching and learning environments, can be constrained by managerial surveillance and market mechanisms of accountability. In the US, Webb (2005) describes the punitive accountability practices of over-surveillance of teachers' work in a case-study school. He suggests that these punitive practices should be replaced with opportunities for teacher education and teacher learning, rather than teacher obedience. Morley (2006) suggests that the acknowledgement of a more professional stance for teachers is more likely to achieve motivation and emotional commitment to the values and needs of the school. In these terms, leaders may wish to move away from over-focus on external audit regimes, which require teachers' to repeatedly prove their competence, and instead allow them to concentrate on sustainable improvement rather than short-term measurable fixes.

The distribution of leadership in schools is thought to be partly driven by the need to address the volume and complexity of work, and partly by a desire to offer professional learning to aspirant leaders so as to build capacity for change and for leadership succession. It has been suggested that distributing leadership to teachers has a positive influence both on teacher effectiveness and on learner engagement (Leithwood and Jantzi, 2000). It has also been suggested that learner outcomes are more likely to improve when leadership sources are distributed throughout the school, enabling teachers to be empowered in areas of importance to them (Silins and Mulford, 2002). Hargreaves and Fink (2006) identify that literature on teacher leadership generally promotes the notion that more teacher leadership will automatically lead to better schools. However, these authors caution that not all teacher leadership is necessarily good leadership. They cite the example that teacher leadership can be bad if it simply encourages teachers to protect their own interests at the expense of student learning. If the distribution of leadership can take a form that leads to the enhanced quality and improvement of the educational experiences of learners in particular schools, then this is likely to attract increased accountability of those empowered to act. MacBeath (2005) suggests that distributing leadership is premised on trust. He points out that while heads may well believe in the importance of trust, they also are aware of the pressure of accountability from external sources and the potential price they themselves must pay if the risk taken in others' leadership goes wrong. In a study involving 11 participating schools, this author uncovered the strength of persistence, associated with longstanding and hierarchical structures and reinforced by accountability mechanisms, that still lead to a focus on change and improvement being located in heads themselves. Despite a growing international interest in the efficacy of student voice in school improvement, this study showed only limited support for the notion of pupils and parents being involved in leadership and decision-making.

To sum up the international nature of the impact of accountability regimes on leaders in education it is useful to examine the work of Leithwood (2001), who explores the implications for leaders of the accountability-driven policy contexts common to schools in many countries and notes four approaches to educational accountability:

- market approaches to accountability;
- decentralization approaches to accountability;
- professional approaches to accountability;
- management approaches to accountability.

As already suggested, in market-based approaches to accountability school leaders are more likely to view learners and their parents as customers, and they may try and engage them, along with other stakeholders, in decision-making aimed at ensuring success and survival in the face of competition from other similar educational organizations. Decentralization tends to imply that stakeholders have been granted the possibility for more decision-making power. A professional approach to accountability acknowledges that teachers are close to learners, so they are potentially well placed to be involved in decision-making related to quality improvements and the raising of standards and attainment. This closeness to learners and the possibility of better targeted decision-making has been partly reflected in the recent international trend of distributing leadership to teachers within schools (Hargreaves and Fink, 2006; MacBeath, 2005; Harris, 2004). A management approach to accountability involves careful planning ideally focused on learner outcomes and it should, therefore, involve dialogue between leaders, managers and teachers. Each of the approaches reviewed by Leithwood requires the engagement of stakeholders and places demands upon school leaders if accountability requirements are to be met. In all cases, a collaborative culture where the trust and involvement of stakeholders has been established appears to offer maximum benefits for learners and presents the best opportunity for data, resources and ideas to be used in school improvement efforts.

Leadership and school improvement

Chapman (2004) has extended this focus on the relationship between leadership and school improvement and in doing so he suggests four central themes for leadership: dispersing leadership; relationships with external agents; the importance of social capital; and the importance of context. Chapman's study revealed that in schools where there were high levels of distributed leadership, professional relationships tended to be more autonomous, potentially favouring more professional approaches to accountability. It was also established that where leadership was seen as more autocratic, with power and control located within the senior team, professional relationships appeared less autonomous, potentially favouring other forms of accountability based on more limited collaboration and trust. Whilst it may be assumed that Ofsted inspection should have a role to play, as part of their accountability and school improvement remit, in initiating positive change in failing schools this may not always be the case. For example, Chapman (2002) showed that in 10 schools facing challenging circumstances, Ofsted inspection led to more autocratic and short-term views on the part of leaders and evoked the view of classroom teaching staff that changes could have been made without the intrusion of Ofsted. There is a view that potentially helpful risk-taking and creativity may be avoided in order to conform to the perceived requirements of Ofsted inspectors (Muijs *et al.*, 2004).

Overall it is clear that the huge change in approaches to accountability education in recent decades has had a major impact on the role of leaders in education, with a movement from a central notion of a leader of learning to the leader as a form of chief executive of a complex financial organization, whose main role is learning. The immense pressures that this has placed on leaders, allied to developments in managerial theory, have led to changing conceptions within educational organizations which suggest that educational institutions should not simply await external audit but that they should proactively seek to monitor quality on a continuous basis. It is to this notion of 'self-review' that we now turn.

Educational institutions' own conceptions of accountability: developing a culture of self-review

The idea that educational institutions should monitor their own performance is not new; there is a long-established tradition of senior leaders and heads of department taking a role in scrutinizing the quality of planning, teaching and outcomes in terms of examination results. However, recent years have witnessed a step change in the understanding of accountability within schools and colleges. The range and depth of internal monitoring and evaluation that is now expected means that a culture of self-review has developed. This approach has increasingly been encouraged by central government agencies. For instance, the Standards Site of the Department for Education and Skills in the UK (DfES, 2005b) offers guidance relating to the practicalities of establishing accountability relationships within Education Improvement Partnerships (see Chapter 7). These are partnerships intended to focus on collaboration between schools, other educational providers (such as colleges) and statutory and voluntary sector organizations to realize benefits and extended service for learners, their families and the community. Members of such partnerships are expected to be collectively accountable for delivering particular services and meeting defined targets. It is suggested that partnership agreements should specify:

- expected inputs, outcomes, monitoring and evaluation processes, as well as procedures which could be taken to rectify any problems;

- the resources available;
- the internal lines of accountability, as partnership members will want clarity among themselves on leadership, management and governance;
- the external lines of accountability, where groups of schools take on responsibility for delivery of named functions from a local authority;
- what action will be taken if individual members fail to contribute as envisaged by the partnership;
- how performance will be managed, perhaps including benchmarking, Ofsted feedback and group performance measures;
- how to minimize bureaucracy to ensure that the benefits from working this way outweigh the costs.

Also in the UK, the Children Act 2005 requires schools to evaluate and account for the extent to which their provision leads to improved outcomes for pupils delineated under the five areas of the *Every Child Matters* agenda (see also Chapter 7). A Department for Education and Skills report (DfES, 2006) presents the results of a survey identifying features of best practice in such self-evaluation. It was recommended that to extend the best practice in self-evaluation, schools, colleges and local authorities should take account of the views of a wide range of stakeholders to inform self-evaluation; use the findings from self-evaluation to inform the priorities in planning for development; and then, focus on self-evaluation, specifically on the impact of provision on the outcomes for children and young people.

A report by McNamara and O'Hara (2006) indicates that evaluating schools and their provision has become a contentious issue in many countries (see also Chapter 8). Disquiet is partly based upon the need to achieve a working balance between evaluation relating to improvement effort, and evaluation required to collect extensive data for public accountability purposes. These authors describe the evolution of an approach to the evaluation of schools in Ireland. The Department of Education and Science in Ireland has issued a framework for school evaluation and self-evaluation (DES, 2003a, 2003b). This framework of self-evaluation is intended to give schools information about their own performance and also to inform inspectors who make whole-school inspections. However, McNamara and O'Hara identify only a very limited role for key stakeholders, particularly parents and students, in the framework. Davis and White (2001) contend that accountability extends beyond only schools themselves being answerable to society, and that the accountability of parents and government for school performance should be included in evaluation. In the case of parents, these authors pose questions about what a community can reasonably expect of good parents with respect to their child's educational development. They also suggested that government itself should be accountable to society for the appropriateness of the educational aims it seeks to promote.

Self-review is not a panacea for educational institutions and such an approach brings with it problems and challenges of its own, not least of which is a vastly increased workload for leaders at all levels. Nonetheless, such an approach is superior to waiting for periodic external review, especially if it is used to turn a spotlight on enhancing approaches to learning and teaching.

Accountability and stakeholders in further education

The material in the previous sections of this chapter has mainly addressed developments in the schools sector. Although the general trend in approaches to accountability has been cross-sector, the nuances of approach make further and higher education worthy of sections on their own. The further education sector reveals many examples of improvements in the curriculum, teaching and learning, and performance relying directly upon the establishment of good working relationships with stakeholders. As in the schools sector, a policy context favouring decentralization and market-based approaches to accountability has prevailed in the UK. Quality assurance has been placed in the hands of the Adult Learning Inspectorate (ALI) and Ofsted, supplemented by college internal self-review (see Chapter 8). As in the schools sector, leaders in further education may view many of their stakeholders as customers and seek to secure on-going patronage, as well as seeking new partnerships to further enhance organizational development and success. Hodkinson and Bloomer (2000b) have argued that institutional accountability for measures of success based on retention and qualification achievement are flawed, as many of the factors that influence retention and qualification completion lie outside the control of the college. Again, parental accountability is raised in such circumstances, especially with respect to younger learners in this sector.

Government, learner and employer dissatisfaction with vocational education, traditionally located within further education, provided the impetus for a Green Paper published in 2002 (DfES, 2002) that set out a proposed route for education reform in this sector with four key goals:

- meeting needs, improving choice;
- putting teaching and learning at the heart of what we do;
- developing the teachers and leaders of the future;
- developing a framework for quality and success.

The Green Paper stated that:

> We need to ensure that learning provided in an area must meet national and local skill needs. It must be responsive to local employers and communities and it must provide young people and adults with the opportunities they need for progression to further and higher education and for employment and personal development.
>
> (DfES, 2002: 8)

Lumby (2001) contends that the choices of young people currently drive the further education system much more strongly than the needs of employers. Indeed, the needs of employers can be perceived as very difficult to establish, given the propensity of some employers to focus on current difficulties rather than taking a longer-term view. Lumby and Wilson (2003) suggest that government belief in building higher-level skills in the present and future workforce in order to create better economic performance is undermined by the competitive strategies of many enterprises, which rely on mass production at the lowest possible cost rather than the high performance of employees.

Although colleges may be accountable to local employers for items such as the bespoke training they provide, accountability for meeting employers' needs at a national level appears to be very much more complex and difficult to define. Simkins and Lumby (2002: 11) describe general and specialist further education colleges as: 'a conglomeration of arenas and players in which culture is contested and negotiated at national, regional and college levels, by managers, lecturers, support staff, and students and by community players such as employers, schools and universities'.

Since the incorporation of the further education sector, or the 'Learning and Skills' sector as it is presently described, in the UK in 1993, research has explored how those in senior posts have set about the task of leading and managing their colleges. Lumby (2002) points out that the available literature generally does not draw on what is known about leadership in schools, rather research has sought to understand the work of colleges as if they were dissociated from other parts of the UK education system. It is clear that more research is needed on the impact of factors on leadership for learning in this sector and how chains of accountability have relationship to quality improvement and raising the outcomes of learners in both academic and vocational endeavours.

Accountability and stakeholders in higher education

The introduction of quality management into higher education has been seen as an international phenomenon. Szanto (2005) highlights the global interest generated by governments and institutions themselves in the quality of their programmes, their reputations and the procedures they have adopted for assuring quality. Huisman and Currie (2004) have identified global trends influencing higher education from the 1980s onwards. These trends include:

- changing relationships between governments and universities;
- efficiency and value for money;
- internationalization of higher education and globalization;
- information and communication technology developments.

In striving to maintain and enhance national and international competitiveness, higher education institutions (HEIs) are subject to a variety of externally imposed quality audit frameworks (see Chapters 1 and 2) and have also introduced internal quality assurance mechanisms, which often reflect items from external frameworks so as to enable report preparation and any necessary remedial activity in advance of external audit visits. Quality assurance agencies responsible for the external quality evaluation of programmes and institutions now operate in most countries throughout the world. Both internal and external quality assurance mechanisms demand the engagement of accountability procedures, and attendant data collection and interpretation relevant to individual institutions. Although students, parents, academics, government, funding bodies, employers and other stakeholders may have differing ideas about what quality in higher education is, the perception of institutional success by stakeholders remains highly important in prestige, student recruitment and economic terms. As in the school and college sectors, the advance of a market-based approach to accountability in higher education has been detectable in recent years. In the UK, for example, information concerning the quality of research, teaching, widening participation, recruitment and retention, and student satisfaction in individual HEIs is now placed in the public domain in order to inform choice and patronage by those seeking to enter the institution and by those the institution seeks to work with.

The importance of partnership with stakeholders clearly has resonance within the higher education sector, and the potential for interaction with stakeholders is vast. In a study involving transition countries, Hendel and Lewis (2005) suggest that accountability relates most strongly to external consumers such as students, benefactors paying fees and the state's provision of financial subsidies. These authors contend that governments seek assurance that HEIs are addressing societal needs by producing the desired graduates as well as generating research and service to improve citizens' lives. Alexander (2000) also points out that accountability focuses on the priorities of stakeholders who have a vested interest in institutional performance. Auditing has been seen as an instrument that can be used to make institutions more formally accountable to their stakeholders. There appears to be an inherent belief that accountability measures can raise the quality of institutional performance by fostering analysis and reflection upon current practices. Auditing is not without its challenges. For example, the quality of teaching in higher education is an important issue for stakeholders that can be accessed indirectly via satisfaction and outcome measures. However, measuring varied student learning experiences as distinct measurable items as a basis for improvement effort could offer distinct challenges across different disciplines. Romzek (2000) emphasizes that professional approaches to accountability are traditionally adopted in HEIs; however, as already mentioned in Chapter 3, external accountability requirements are contributing to a more managerialist stance by manager-academics within the sector. Hoecht (2006) has suggested the possibility that governments, increasingly faced with decreasing trust from electors, have advocated audit measures to make the public institutions more accountable and hence to enhance the portrayal of politicians as guardians of the public interest.

Despite the attention paid to external whole institutional or programme inspections which place information within the public domain, there is still much kudos to be gained by individual academics from their success in publication and gaining funding awards. Success in this peer-reviewed professional area also has benefits in terms of reputation and additional funding for the host universities themselves. Leaders and managers in higher education need to be cognizant of the contributions made by individual talent to their public image.

In Chapter 4, the work of Oldroyd (2005) was used to distinguish between two dimensions of human resource management (HRM): hard HRM which displays a managerialist tendency and soft HRM which is more concerned with professional autonomy and empowerment. Caught in a tension between the application of soft HRM approaches, with few sanctions, to foster a more collegial and collaborative environment and the application of hard HRM approaches, seeking to translate accountability policies into institutional mechanisms for data collection and account,

Huisman and Currie (2004) suggest that the weakest link in the accountability chain in higher education may be higher education management itself. However, accountability and professional autonomy are not mutually exclusive and academic freedom must not be mistaken for independence resulting in lack of accountability. However, tensions do remain. For example, in a case-study university in the UK, Coyle (2003) examined the balance between autonomy and accountability in one university's quality management system. In developing its quality system this university experimented with a customer-centred model to place the needs of stakeholders at the heart of its planning, operation and evaluations. Indeed, Coyle suggests that this shift in balance between provider and customer perspective is a further recognition of the increasing public accountability placed on HEIs in the UK. The case study showed that managers and other staff found not only were there competing differences between the desires of various stakeholders, but also that the associated self-evaluation within the university, with its requirement for annual monitoring, sparked criticism from academics perceiving an over-surveillance and over-accountability associated with the shift from autonomy towards annual reporting. It is concluded that such customer-centred approaches demand high levels of leadership and management skill if an acceptable balance between professional autonomy and accountability is to be maintained.

Conclusion

This chapter served to illustrate the wide variety and complexity of relationships between internal and external stakeholders and host organizations in the school, further and higher education sectors. Educational organizations are accountable to their stakeholders for their efficiency, effectiveness, equity and performance and leaders and managers are important mediators of transactions resulting from stakeholder relationships including the reconciliation of differing perspectives of audit and quality held by different stakeholders.

A market-based approach to accountability has become more prevalent and this has more firmly linked institutional performance to public image and all that this entails. The chapter indicated that responsiveness to context, and the professionality and professionalism of staff are influential in approaches to accountability and quality enhancement. What is clear is that short-term targets that are quickly and easily measured for the purposes of accountability ought not to dominate longer term visions of sustainable improvement and enhanced learner outcomes.

Intrusive external evaluation is seen by some educationalists as demoralizing and de-professionalizing for teachers, who may seek improvement based upon professional autonomy and professional accountability rather than on control. Leadership and management have the possibility to foster more democratic and professional approaches to autonomy and accountability in the face of any feelings of constraining control and sanction which may detract from necessary passion to effect improvement efforts leading to enhanced learner outcomes. School leaders may consider the promotion of more collaborative, trusting and reflective environments in order to mediate between political demands and the experiences of professionals in schools.

Nevertheless, they are accountable for their organizational performance to demanding stakeholders and may face the dilemma of having to choose between soft and hard approaches to HRM in order to best serve the prescribed and expected levels of performance demanded of them.

School leaders increasingly need to understand their role in facilitating and directing a network of relationships both inside and outside the school if they are to attain the best possible outcomes for the learners in their care. For example, in both the UK and in other countries, schools can be seen as important foci for community cohesion as well as institutions offering credentials for future work and continuing education. For these reasons, as well as fostering a community culture supportive of higher expectation with respect to learner inclusion and outcomes (see Chapter 3), the establishment of good home–school links is essential. In some schools this may constitute an important element in the work of leaders and managers, given the possible disenfranchisement of individuals and groups of learners and their families.

In the further education sector, measures of accountability that draw on items such as student completion and retention may evoke questions concerning the true locus of responsibility if students do not complete courses, as in some cases this may not fall within the control of colleges themselves. This sector is under-researched, but it is clear that the demands of market accountability pertain within this sector, as they do in the schools sector. Both internal and external audits of quality (see Chapters 8 and 9) seek to assess stakeholder satisfaction and institutional performance as a basis for further improvement. In higher education internal and external evaluation, as part of quality assurance and control, are increasingly established as commonplace. There is abundant evidence of the desire of leaders and managers to ensure good subject and institutional performance, given the impact of market accountability and the attendant concern about the outcomes of audit and their influence upon recruitment and funding. A particular challenge for leadership and management in this sector is achieving a balance between traditional professional autonomy and approaches to accountability that indicate a trend of increasing managerialism. Overall, more studies of leadership and management in contemporary settings located within this sector are needed, so that robust conceptual frameworks can inform the linkage of leadership and stakeholder engagement to the best interests of all learners in their care.

7 Relationships with stakeholders

Introduction

This chapter seeks to further explore the complex sets of relationships that educational leaders must manage if their institutions are to be successful. These relationships include parents, students and local and national government authorities. In commercial contexts, the term 'stakeholder' refers to any group or individual who has legitimate expectation of a company. Stakeholders can include stockholders, employees, customers, suppliers, creditors, managers, the local community, special interest groups, the general public, government and any other groups that have entered into a relationship with the company. Being aware of the range of stakeholders and their relative power, companies actively seek to satisfy the needs and expectations of their stakeholders in order to ensure survival and success (Dobson and Starkey, 1993).

This chapter maintains a focus on the education sector and the leadership and management of relationships with stakeholders, so that quality and outcomes can be enhanced. Although the field is potentially vast, the chapter maintains an overall focus on learners as stakeholders. To this end, issues pertaining to learners themselves, parents, community, school and university partnerships and the drive to widen participation are explored. Managing such relationships presents a variety of challenges for leaders and managers as they seek to maximize benefits for their organizations and their learners and strive to remediate or minimize any disadvantages preventing improvement. In this chapter we examine:

- stakeholders and quality improvement in schools;
- the role of the headteacher or principal in managing stakeholder relationships;
- parents as partners;
- stakeholders and quality improvement.

Much of the discussion on the topics noted earlier is based on the literature relating specifically to schools, and separate sections are also included on relationships with stakeholders in the latter phases of education. Thus, we also examine:

- stakeholders and quality in further education;
- stakeholders and quality in higher education.

We conclude by emphasizing that in all sectors, stakeholder engagement and satisfaction represents an important investment in the virtuous circle of quality enhancement.

Stakeholders and quality improvement in schools

The importance of learning-centred leadership in schools (see Chapter 5) has already received much attention in the research literature and it has been seen to have great potential in developing and sustaining school improvement and effectiveness (Benson, 2002; Hollingsworth, 2004; Southworth, 2004; Webb, 2005). Dimmock (2000) sees a learning-centred school as one whose mission, organization, curriculum and leadership are focused on providing successful learning experiences and outcomes for pupils. In a strategic approach to improving pupil learning outcomes, Dimmock and Walker (2004) suggest that the starting point for leadership should be to identify the nature and quality of learning outcomes sought by the school. This is then followed by a backward-mapping process to consider appropriate changes to learning processes and experiences, teaching strategies and methods, organizational structures and the socio-cultural environment that will be required to provide the identified learning outcomes. In attempting to lead and manage the socio-cultural environment, it is certain that productive partnerships with both internal and external stakeholders who have an interest in the school, such as parents, pupils, staff and the community will need to be secured and directed towards improvement efforts. Busher (1998) has depicted the external constituencies of a school as including, for example, local social and community groups and local and central policy-makers and employers. He describes the internal constituencies of a school as including pupils, teachers, support staff, parents and governors. Glatter (1997) points out that how the internal processes of schools are influenced by their external environments has been poorly researched. However, some of the complexity of interaction between the external and internal environments is identified by Busher (2006) who points out that all members of a school have contact with the external environment. For example, pupils and school staff may well live in local communities and the views about the school they express in their communities can affect the way in which the school is generally perceived (see Busher and Saran, 2000). Many authors have suggested that students' home influences have much greater impact on the outcome of their schooling than does the effective management of schools (Creemers, 1994; Mortimore and Whitty, 1997; Lauder and Hughes, 1999). It is, however, incumbent upon school leaders to create and manage these partnership boundaries to best effect in order to maximize advantage and minimize disadvantage for the organization and for their learners.

The role of the headteacher or principal in managing stakeholder relationships

As already indicated, the head or principal of a school is most likely to be central to the management of boundaries and cross-boundary transactions between internal and external stakeholders. In the UK, the *National Standards for Headteachers* (DfES, 2004a) establishes that the key purpose of the head is to provide professional leadership and management for the school as a basis upon which to secure high standards in all areas of the school's work. Extracts from the *National Standards* emphasize the perceived importance of managing the relationships with stakeholders, including those located in the local community. Strategies are required for:

- communication within and beyond the school;
- monitoring and self-evaluation;
- performance evaluation and management;
- developing good interpersonal relationships;
- building and sustaining a learning community;
- collaborating with others in order to strengthen the school's organizational capacity;
- stakeholder and community engagement in, and accountability for, the success and celebration of the school's performance;
- engaging with the internal and external school community to secure equity and entitlement;
- collaboration with other schools to share expertise;
- collaboration both strategically and operationally with parents and carers and multiple agencies for the well-being of all children;
- awareness that school improvement and community development are interdependent;
- knowledge of the diverse physical and human resources within local communities;
- knowledge of the work of other agencies and opportunities for collaboration;
- encouraging parents and carers to support their children's learning;
- listening to and reflecting and acting upon community feedback.

(DfES, 2004a: 7)

In these terms, the school becomes a potentially charged meeting place for the presentation, negotiation and consensual acceptance of the interests and expectations of a large number of people associated with the school, drawn from both the internal and external environments in which the school operates. This complex forum demands high levels of commitment, stamina and emotional resilience on the part of heads in all schools, and the likelihood of increased demands where individual schools face special or challenging circumstances. In a study of 10 successful heads who had all raised levels of measurable pupil attainments in their schools and were all regarded highly by their peers, Day (2004) showed that all these heads revealed a passion for education, for pupils and for the communities in which they worked. This passion for pupils, school and community was thought fundamental to the achievement of success and emphasized the need for intellectual and emotional engagement with all stakeholders. There is clearly no single approach that heads may, or should, adopt to respond to given groups of stakeholders in the same way. For example, Coleman and Earley (2005) suggest that how leaders and managers in schools and colleges respond to the variability, diversity and complexity of the parents, families and communities they serve depends, in part, on their ideas of how they can best participate. They may be seen as:

- customers in a competitive market;
- citizens with rights expressed through governorship and quality assurance models;
- clients to be offered professional expertise;
- first educators of their own children;
- partners in which adults and professionals work together.

In the US, Van Voorhis and Sheldon (2004) have explored the importance of the school principal in developing school, family, and community partnerships. The study draws on previous research showing that parental and community involvement can improve student outcomes, improve student retention and attendance and reduce drop-out rates, improve student behaviour, improve student access to physical and social services and foster youth and adult relationships. The results suggest the key importance of engaging the principal in partnership formation, monitoring, evaluation and expansion of partnerships rather than leaving it to individual teachers to promote student success and development in this way. Also in the US, Sanders and Lewis (2005) have confirmed that in three case studies of high schools with successful community partnerships, the leaders' motivation for community partnership development was based on a desire to improve learners' academic and personal success, enhance school quality and support community development.

Parents as partners

As mentioned in Chapter 6, many educationalists are drawn to the idea of parents as partners. In the UK, for example, Bastiani (2002) has created a framework to improve school or college relationships with parents, families and the community. In evaluating the quality of home–school links, MacBeath (1999) suggests the following indicators are of importance and point the way to possible interventions on the part of leadership and management as a basis to improve quality and learner outcomes:

- parents play an active role in their children's learning;
- parents are confident that problems will be dealt with and feedback given;
- the school provides for the social, cultural and linguistic backgrounds of pupils;
- parent–teacher meetings are useful and productive;
- pupil progress is monitored and shared with parents on a regular basis.

The improvement of home–school links requires leadership committed to the idea that this will have advantages for learners, either directly or indirectly through parental support and the perceptions of education that pupils bring into school with them (see also Chapter 9). Such views and perceptions may be expressed in pupils' behaviour and engagement in school activities, and hence impact upon their own and others' experiences of teaching and learning. Some studies have shown that the deployment of teaching and learning support assistants has helped in fostering positive home–school links and the inclusion of some of the most challenging pupils (Rhodes, 2006). The literature reveals a number of examples of the positive impact of links between home and teaching assistants to effect pupil inclusion. For example, Logan and Feiler (2006) report on a successful Literacy Early Action Project (LEAP). This is a home-based project to involve parents in their children's learning through the deployment of teaching assistants so as to raise attainment in the literacy of children who were considered to be least likely to thrive in the reception year of primary school.

Involvement in a child's education is widely viewed as a key parental responsibility, impacting on the child's future well-being and life chances. This involvement may be difficult to achieve in some cases. Indeed, a study by Crozier and Davies (2007) emphasized some of the difficulties that schools may have in engaging parents, and that parents themselves may experience in becoming more involved in their children's learning. Pinkus (2006) reports on obstacles that continue to hinder the achievement of good working relationships between parents and professionals. This author contends that this may be heightened for parents located within ethnic minority communities. According to the current UK government, inadequate parenting is driving a cycle of deprivation characterized by poverty, low aspiration and anti-social behaviour (see Gillies, 2005). An analysis by Gillies (2006) goes on to suggest that parental involvement in academic success involves an emotional commitment that members of the middle class are more traditionally willing to make, resulting in better future prospects for their children. In contrast, it is suggested that this is much less the case for working class mothers, whose involvement in school life is likely to be more orientated towards ensuring that their children are safe, combating feelings of failure and low self-worth and challenging perceptions of injustice. For school leaders and managers, such diversity of perspective, even within one group of stakeholders, presents considerable challenges in their work to manage partnership boundaries in order to maximize learner advantage.

Attempts have been made in some schools, through mechanisms such as parents' consultation groups, pupils' councils and the engagement of pupil voice (see Chapter 5), to involve learners and their parents in decision-making and school improvement activities. Indeed, Joyce *et al.* (1999: 56) have suggested that an 'active, living democracy, including community members, engaged in collective inquiry, creates the structural conditions in which the process of school improvement is nested'. However, despite progress made in some schools, Day (2003) contends that over the last two decades in the UK the discourses of school effectiveness and school improvement, aimed at raising standards within a framework of market accountability, have been accommodated more readily by middle-class communities; these discourses have only served to further disadvantage many inner-city, migrant and socially deprived communities.

Leaders need to recognize differences in power between stakeholder individuals and groups, as it is likely that the most powerful individuals and groups will be most influential in asserting their views. Acknowledgement of power differences between stakeholders has emerged in some overseas contexts. For example, in an international study of developing countries, Khan (2006) suggests that when governments decentralize education in developing countries, one response is to increase community participation by establishing school councils that include parents and other community representatives. It is assumed that community participation will improve democratic governance and accountability. Local communities are thought to have the potential to reverse declining standards through their governance, improve the quality of facilities, increase enrolment and attendance, and adopt curricula that are relevant to the local needs of the whole community. However, in some countries a predominance of affluent and educated members of the community have become members of school councils at the expense of poor and less well-educated individuals, who are therefore less well represented. Khan concludes that parents who are more educated are more likely to interact with school directors and teachers and be far more vocal in decision-making than less advantaged and powerful individuals. In many countries the notion of community is developing and shifting as demographics change and new shared interests emerge. One example of community change of significance to schools in the UK is offered by the growing multicultural nature of educational institutions and the need to acknowledge and respond to this diversity (Shah, 2004). In a more recent work, Shah (2006) draws attention to an Islamic perspective of educational leadership and its linkage to the perception of leadership by Muslim students in all phases of education. These perspectives are discussed in relation to students' likely performance and achievement in British educational organizations. It is suggested that multidirectional knowledge-sharing can assist societal cohesion, as well as improving practice and students' educational performance. The requirement of school leaders to deal with the tensions between managerialism and care, accountability and professional autonomy, competition and collaboration, the needs of diverse learners and the narrow instrumentalism of government required 'standards' (Gewirtz *et al.*, 1995) continues to present challenges to schools both in the UK and internationally.

Higher education institutions (HEIs) have increasingly become involved as stakeholders in schools (for example, see Rhodes *et al.*, 2005). Proponents of teachers as school-based educational researchers (Stenhouse, 1975; Carr and Kemmis, 1986) have long seen action research in classrooms as a stimulant to reflection, improvement and professional development. Perhaps the best known recent initiative in the UK was the launch of Best Practice Research Scholarships by the Department for Education and Skills in 2000. Typically, participating teachers were supported by academics from HEIs, so that they might secure insights into educational research methods. In developing such partnerships, Catelli *et al.* (2000) have asked who benefits from the action research, the school, the teacher or the academics themselves. There have also been repeated concerns that school-based research is becoming small-scale problem-solving in nature, with an attendant failure to develop wider theoretical perspectives (Avis, 2001; Bartlett, 2002), and that teachers are often wary of theory unless it can be demonstrated that it has some clear relevance to their own work. This theory–practice divide stands as a potential barrier to collaboration between school and HEI staff in potential improvement-based collaborations. It is a divide which needs to be carefully managed if true collaborative partnerships between schools and HEIs are to be established, rather than limited associations characterized by objectives and agendas which are overtly distinct. Partnership requires academics to avoid insensitive approaches in which they colonize school knowledge and impose their own research models (Gore and Gitlin, 2004). The power dynamics that frame school-based research should seek interaction appropriate to the benefit of both partners if collaboration is to succeed and be sustainable. Until recently, Networked Learning Communities of teachers engaged in inquiry-based learning and practitioner research have been supported financially in England, and such networking has been promoted by the National College for School Leadership. Sharing research findings and improvement ideas has the potential to foster teachers' learning from one another in professional learning communities and networks and hence contribute to individual school improvement journeys (Bolam *et al.*, 2005).

Stakeholders and quality improvement

A raft of central government legislation and initiatives has emerged in the UK to further extend and engage stakeholders active in supporting quality improvement and enhanced learner inclusion and outcomes in schools. These changes have significant implications for the future leadership and management of schools. For example, the UK Education Act 2002 requires schools to consult with pupils, staff, parents and carers, local communities and the local authority to ensure that services they develop are shaped around the needs of the pupils and their local community. Governing bodies are seen to have a key role in consulting with communities. A central government expectation that schools should become 'extended schools' has arisen. Extended schools potentially offer a range of services to meet the needs of children, families and the local community. For example, schools may provide high-quality childcare, open facilities, and referral to specialist services, as well as activities such as homework clubs, music tuition, sport, and languages (TDA, 2006b). Extended services can be organized directly by a school or in partnership with private or voluntary sector providers. The leadership and management of extension, allowing community access to school facilities, can be seen as beneficial in terms of maximizing use of facilities, achieving income from use of facilities, improved parent and community involvement with schools, an improved sense of community and adult learning opportunities. If these services are taken up by community members, the potential for impact directly or indirectly upon pupil achievement is self-evident.

The Department for Education and Skills in the UK has offered a prospectus concerning the formation of Education Improvement Partnerships (DfES, 2005b). It is suggested that these partnerships should be focused on good quality collaboration between schools, further education colleges, other educational providers, and other statutory and voluntary sector organizations. The UK government suggests that Educational Improvement Partnerships have potential benefits in a variety of contexts including 14–19 provision, personalization of provision (see Chapter 5), behaviour improvement and the development of childcare and extended services. It is also proposed that Education Improvement Partnerships can assist schools in gaining multi-agency support and hence be of value in the delivery of the five outcomes of the *Every Child Matters* agenda (DfES, 2003b):

- being healthy;
- staying safe;
- enjoying and achieving;

- making a positive contribution;
- achieving economic well-being in life.

The leadership and management of such partnerships will need to be able to establish details of communication, resource use, monitoring and evaluation, internal lines of accountability, external lines of accountability, performance management and bureaucracy reduction if they are to function efficiently and effectively.

Stakeholders and quality in further education

Partnership with stakeholders such as parents, community, employers and higher education has strong resonance within the further education sector in the UK, as it does in schools. There are many examples of curriculum, teaching and learning, improvement and performance relying directly upon the establishment of good working relationships with stakeholders. Kelly *et al.* (2005) acknowledge the importance of internal partnerships between college leadership and college staff. For example, as in schools, leadership in the college sector is now very much concerned with gaining the trust of organizational members, so that capacity for change can be built. Overall, these authors suggest that, if improvement and better learning outcomes are to be achieved, leadership in colleges should be increasingly about the successful organization of a complex network of distributed leadership practices involving staff from across the organization.

Liaison with employers in some schools may be centred on gaining short work-placement experience for pupils; however, given the overt vocational nature of some further education provision, there is a long history of employer involvement within the sector. A major development was the establishment of the National Council for Vocational Qualifications in 1986, intended to introduce a nationally recognized system of vocational qualifications into the UK. The resulting National Vocational Qualifications (NVQs) were designed to enable individuals to show competence in vocational skills, coupled with development of an appropriate underlying knowledge base. These qualifications were designed to be undertaken partly in college, but mainly within the individual's own workplace. The work-based approach of NVQs required close liaison between further education colleges and employers. College staff were given an extended tutoring role because the students were off-site in their workplace for substantial periods. The assessment of NVQs was intended to be undertaken partly by college staff and partly by employers in the workplace. If work-based assessment was required of employers, then the employer or other work-based staff were trained to undertake this assessment. McCrystal and McAleer (2003) have examined the management of NVQs by colleges of further education and higher education 10 years after their introduction in Northern Ireland. The findings report positive benefits from working in collaboration with employers. However, it is concluded that more work is needed to improve the working relationships between colleges and employers at all levels of NVQ delivery.

The Kennedy report (1997) argued that if further education is to fulfil its potential in terms of widening learner participation it needs to ensure wide involvement on the part of employers and members of the community. Further education was seen to have an important role to play in lifelong learning developments, seeking to bridge the learning divide between those who have received the benefits of education and training and those who have not (DfEE, 1998c). To this end, it was suggested that members of further education college governing bodies should be drawn from key stakeholder groups including business, local government, community, college staff, students and parents (DfEE, 1998d). The scope of sector activities and their actual and potential interaction with a wide variety of stakeholders is vast. Gravatt and Silver (2000) emphasized that college principals need to be aware of the diversity within their local communities and work with them so as to open the doors to community access and partnership. Similarly, Hyland and Merrill (2001), in examining the key question of the purposes of further education, suggest the importance of careful knowledge of the community of stakeholders with their diverse needs and interests. Stakeholder partnership raises the possibility of quality improvement, social inclusion and also economic income. Colleges may face serious tensions between local and regional, social and community needs and the economic pressures reflected in the need to remain financially viable. For example, Hyland and Matlay (1998) raise the paradox of local small businesses who may be happy with the standard of training available at their local college, but cannot afford the time and cost of sending employees to the college on a regular basis. The management of such tensions invites innovative and entrepreneurial solutions within prevailing audit and policy contexts.

Stakeholders and quality in higher education

The importance of managing stakeholder relationships is also well-established in the higher education sector. For example, large-scale surveys have consistently shown that when young people are considering entry to higher education the advice of parents is very influential in decisions about access and choice (Brooks, 2004). Another example is reflected in the growing interest in staff transformational leadership within classrooms as a basis for further work concerning improvement and quality (Pounder, 2006).

The potential for interaction with stakeholders is vast and includes many external organizations, such as those who are involved in the funding of research and consultancy both nationally and internationally. Given that understandings of partnership and collaboration may vary and notwithstanding possible power differences between partners, collaborative partnership is seen as potentially helpful if there is mutual benefit for stakeholders, perhaps reflected in a positive change in process, product or output (Tett *et al.*, 2003). Trust between stakeholders and individuals is the glue of sustainability (Clegg and McNulty, 2002; Milbourne *et al.*, 2003). The dynamism of working with a partner can be a strong motivator for staff and the benefits can help further develop staff, students and the organizational culture. Against a backdrop of UK government desire for linkages between higher education and employers, Foskett (2005) has examined the extrinsic pressure for institutions to work within collaborative partnerships and its effect on curriculum change in higher education. The author thus offers a model that could underpin and enhance collaborative partnerships within the higher education sector.

Government policies for higher education in the UK over the last two decades have been influenced by a belief that higher education can contribute to economic prosperity, hence such policies have encouraged the development of work-related curricula within higher education (Little, 2005). A growing trend towards vocationalism within the higher education curriculum, with an attendant promotion of the needs of employers and the workplace, has become more evident (Saunders and Machell, 2000). In 2000, the UK government supported the emergence of employer-led foundation degrees, aimed at improving the delivery of technical and professional skills to meet industry and business needs. In the US, Person and Rosenbaum (2006) have sought to establish if links with employers might influence educational outcomes in occupational programs in private and public colleges. It was concluded that these links can further motivate students, especially if they lead to actual placement in jobs. It was also concluded that faculty and college links to employers can give students concrete benefits in the labour market, which can improve their future job success. On this basis, these authors advocate that leadership and management should further improve links to employers.

A number of studies have attempted to explore the barriers to participation of non-traditional groups of students as stakeholders in higher education (Marks, 2000; Watt and Patterson, 2000; Connor, 2001; Rhodes *et al.*, 2002). It is insufficient that non-traditional groups merely gain access to higher education; they must also stay, progress and achieve success in qualification completion. Hence, there has been a proliferation of research concerned with student retention driven by social and equity concerns as well as the economic considerations of securing enrolments (Peterson *et al.*, 1997; Ozga and Sukhnandan, 1998; Yorke, 2000; Palmer, 2001; Bennett, 2003; Laing and Robinson, 2003). The reasons for student drop-out and withdrawal are complex, and difficulties in translating explanatory models derived in the US to the UK context have been identified (Ozga and Sukhnandan, 1998; Laing and Robinson, 2003). Bennett (2003) establishes some unifying themes within the literature related to drop-out and withdrawal: student satisfaction, motivation, self-esteem, academic performance, integration, financial and other personal problems. Rhodes and Nevill (2004) have explored the relationship with student stakeholders in terms of academic and social integration in a new university setting in the UK for both 'traditional' and 'non-traditional' students. Academic and social integration are both potentially influential in student retention and success in universities. It was found that emergent themes pertained to teaching and learning, debt and other money worries, workload and support. It was concluded that many of the facets of student concern fall within institutional control and could be managed, so that traditional and non-traditional students may have a greater likelihood of achieving integration, maintain their personal vision and be retained.

Establishing that institutional systems aimed at ensuring recruitment efforts, such as marketing (see Chapter 6), are not undermined by misplaced retention efforts is likely to be an increasingly important aspect of university life. Early warnings of retention difficulties within cohorts may help direct institutional leadership and management actions to secure better academic and social integration for all students. Institutions should seek knowledge of key stress points, such as induction, post-induction and first assessment. Pertaining to student recruitment, retention and success, the emergence of a shift in the higher education cost burden from governments (or taxpayers) to parents and students is a worldwide trend reflected in the introduction of increases in tuition fees and in the diminution of student grants (Johnstone, 2004). The full effects of fee introduction in UK universities are yet to be realized and may lead to a shifting of the dynamics of the relationship between student stakeholders and their universities in terms of a greater propensity to litigation if their customer needs are deemed not to have been fully realized. Overall, in this sector, failure to recruit target student numbers, or other funding reductions, have a relatively quick and possibly highly damaging effect on institutional income. In the competition for the best students, poor quality ratings advertised in the public domain can lead to a potentially disastrous downward spiral of falling student numbers, falling income, and a worsening national and international reputation. Academic jobs may well be put at risk. Leaders and managers have become highly sensitive to changes that may affect their institutions in this way (Temple, 2006) and concern themselves with efforts related to quality assurance and quality enhancement so as to meet the expectations of existing and potential stakeholders.

Conclusion

The variety of possible stakeholders within individual organizations is potentially very large and creating an appropriate range of mutually trusting partnerships with stakeholders in order to support improvement and success has become very important for all organizations. It is clear that some stakeholder groups, for example, parents, learners, teaching staff, community and employers are common across all sectors. The recruitment and retention of learner stakeholders is clearly closely related to immediate financial income, and the failure to achieve good management of such stakeholder interests can lead to dire consequences for continued organizational success, and even organizational survival. In these terms, notions of the importance of quality assurance, quality enhancement and meeting the needs of stakeholders will be drawn to the minds of managers and leaders in all educational organizations.

In UK schools, a holistic view of the education and well-being of children has emerged and is expressed via the *Every Child Matters* agenda (DfES, 2003b), which is itself dependent upon partnership with new stakeholders. The full impact of these new partnerships, in terms of challenge to existing school leadership models, has yet to be fully realized. Whilst all sectors are aware of the importance of stakeholders in achieving financial viability, tensions can occur between the desire for altruistic community involvement and the need to secure sufficient income, since there are those who feel that all core functions of educational institutions should be paid for by central government. In the higher education sector, manager-academics are increasingly charged with establishing 'accreditation' arrangements with external partners, consultancy and efforts to gain research funding as well as securing buoyant student numbers across the organization's portfolio. In all sectors, leadership and management action to facilitate stakeholder engagement and satisfaction represents an important investment in the virtuous circle of quality enhancement, leading to present success and, in turn, to future success.

Part III

Impact and prospect in quality and accountability

8 Internal evaluation and review

Introduction

The key focus of this chapter is the use of self-evaluation mechanisms in schools, colleges and in higher education organizations and the efficacy of these mechanisms in bringing about quality improvement and the enhancement of learner outcomes. The use of such mechanisms involves the generation and analysis of data by the organization relevant to its own functioning and improvement. Self-evaluation is now described as a 'mainstream concept', adopted by most education systems throughout Europe (McNamara and O'Hara, 2008). Information arising from such evaluation may assist the organization in improvement activities, but evaluation is also required to provide information for public accountability purposes. McNamara and O'Hara (2006) rightly ask how the balance between these two objectives can be achieved. More specifically, in this chapter we examine:

- the international trend towards autonomy in school management;
- external evaluation versus self-evaluation;
- accountability and self-evaluation;
- improvement and self-evaluation.

Although there are great commonalities between concepts of internal evaluation and review in all stages of education, we consider that there are sufficient nuances to require a separate consideration of each phase. For this reason we also provide sections on:

- self-evaluation and schools in the UK;
- self-evaluation and further education;
- self-evaluation and higher education.

We conclude by suggesting that leaders should not neglect the potential of self-evaluation at all levels within their organization.

The international trend towards autonomy in school management

As already mentioned in this text, enhanced school autonomy, resulting from decentralization, has become a trend that is evident in many countries (Coleman and Earley,

2005). In the UK, the decentralization of schools (Bullock and Thomas, 1997) and the incorporation of colleges (Ainley and Bailey, 1997) have been put forward as a means of allowing greater organizational autonomy in strategic and financial decision-making, intended to lead to improved outcomes for learners. Indeed, Reezigt and Creemers (2005) cite the autonomy granted to schools as a major support for improvement and suggest that external evaluation and accountability act as significant pressures upon schools to improve. In short, in many European countries decentralization has meant an increased pressure on schools to understand what is meant by quality in education and to become more accountable via regular public evaluation of their work. Organizational accountability for public funds and for high professional standards of service for stakeholders, including learners, has become the reverse side of the autonomy coin. According to one view, the resultant impact on leaders and managers within educational organizations has been described as the rise of a 'new normality' (Hoyle and Wallace, 2005), where school leaders have become the conduits for centrally generated educational reforms and teachers the 'deliverers' of changed practices, as more exacting accountability to government and to other stakeholders is demanded.

The debate in many countries has been about the best approaches to school improvement, with the emergence of a continuum characterized at one extreme by tight external control and inspection and at the other by self-evaluation and internal regulation. McNamara and O'Hara illustrate this dichotomy between internal quality assessment and external quality control:

> ... schools and teachers will become more autonomous, taking greater responsibility for budgets, planning, self-evaluation and professional development. Somewhat paradoxically, however, to ensure accountability in the form of the maintenance and indeed constant improvement of standards, these same schools and teachers are to be the subject of sophisticated surveillance procedures including teacher-proof curricula, increased student testing, benchmarking, inspection and external evaluation.
>
> (McNamara and O'Hara, 2008: 173)

In practice, most countries have moved to a combination of internal and external evaluation to underpin improvement and accountability. Externally imposed evaluation has become associated with inspection regimes, whereas internal self-evaluation, if collegial and non-threatening, has become associated with organizational development and improvement. For example, in Finnish schools, Webb *et al.* (1998) have shown that self-evaluation has had positive impacts in improving classroom practices and MacBeath (1999) has suggested that self-evaluation has a role to play in organizational development, in improving teaching and learning and that it can also be used for accountability purposes. This chapter explores issues concerning the balance between internal and external evaluation, the relationship between self-evaluation and accountability and improvement and also issues pertaining to self-evaluation located within the schools, college and higher education sectors. The chapter concludes with some of the emergent drivers and barriers to self-evaluation as a contributory mechanism to quality improvement and raised learner outcomes within educational organizations.

External evaluation versus self-evaluation

Evaluation implies a systematic assessment of what has been achieved within a specified timeframe in relation to stated original aims. Evaluation informs any following actions, and seeks improvements if any shortcomings are identified. Given that external evaluation may be perceived by teachers as judgemental and controlling, and that self-evaluation is often perceived as a less-threatening developmental process, what should be the balance between the two? (see Livingston and McCall, 2005). In addressing such a question, Nevo (2001) also asks the question, can external and internal evaluations live together? In conclusion he advocates that both types are needed as they both have important roles to play. For example, if schools were able to participate as equal partners in external evaluations they would potentially gain greater benefit from the experience and internal evaluation has potentially positive implications for teacher professionalization. Overall, a synergistic relationship is proposed between internal and external evaluation, in which external evaluation stimulates and legitimizes the validity of internal evaluation and internal evaluation increases the awareness of external evaluation to local context. In an attempt to reconcile external evaluation and self-evaluation and to realize the potential benefits of both, it has been suggested for some time that external inspection should incorporate data from self-evaluation and self-identified areas for improvement as a means to overcome the limitations of external inspection (see Ferguson *et al.*, 2000).

As this chapter will show, self-evaluation has now begun to impact to a greater or lesser degree upon the prominence of inspection procedures in many countries. Meanwhile, self-evaluation mechanisms have encompassed the need to serve accountability as well as improvement efforts. For example, using Scottish case studies, Livingston and McCall (2005) have explored ways in which schools, through their internal self-evaluation processes, may use data to meet many of the external demands placed upon them. In Belgium the school inspectorate encourages schools to undertake self-evaluation both in preparation for inspection and also as a means to protect quality, as it is acknowledged that external evaluation does not mean that quality assurance is guaranteed (see Devos and Verhoeven, 2003). These authors defend the role of inspectors as 'critical friends' who can help to discover a school's self-evaluation blind spots and point to them for school leaders to address any identified areas for improvement. In Ireland, demands from parents and other stakeholders for greater transparency and accountability with respect to schools and schooling has led to an emphasis on school self-evaluation (McNamara and O'Hara, 2005). The Department for Education and Science in Ireland (DES, 2003a; 2003b) has emphasized a policy for school self-evaluation as a preparation for inspection and also as a driver of internal school change and improvement, stating: 'Ireland is adopting a model of quality assurance that emphasizes school development planning through internal school review and self-evaluation with the support of external evaluation carried out by the Inspectorate' (DES, 2003b: viii).

Overall, self-evaluation in schools appears to offer a potentially powerful approach to quality auditing. Indeed, MacBeath (1999) lists the possible purposes of self-evaluation as including accountability, staff professional development, whole organizational development and the improvement of teaching and learning.

Accountability and self-evaluation

As already intimated, the balance between external evaluation and self-evaluation is still emerging in some countries and in some sectors of education. However, there has been some disquiet expressed about the place of self-evaluation with respect to accountability and concern that externally imposed accountability requirements, with a high focus on measurable outcomes to be reported in the public domain, may become over dominant at the expense of school improvement (see Rudd and Davis, 2000). For example, Hargreaves and Hopkins (1994: 3) have suggested: 'When accountability is seen as the major instrument for promoting school effectiveness, development planning, originally designed to assist schools in their growth towards greater effectiveness, could lose all its potential as a means of school improvement'.

Leithwood (1999) has suggested that accountability policies can be grouped into four different categories, which he identifies as market approaches, decentralized approaches, professional approaches and management approaches. Leithwood (2001) used these four categories to explore the implications for leaders of the accountability-driven policy contexts found in schools in many countries at that time. Leithwood's (2001) work suggests four approaches including:

1. *Market approaches* where the leader needs to create a marketable product with a clear mission, develop good customer relations, and respond quickly to changing market conditions.
2. *Decentralized approaches* where the leader needs to engage parents and other stakeholders in providing feedback and making decisions, encourage power-sharing and the distribution of leadership and be skilled in resource management.
3. *Professional approaches* where the leader needs to create a learning community, distribute leadership, know about best practices, assist staff in identifying appropriate standards for their work, set expectations and monitor progress.
4. *Management approaches* where the leader needs to engage strategic management, be skilled in collecting and interpreting data and manage the planning process.

The research literature shows examples where accountability measures have been portrayed as a means to achieve equity. For example, Flinders (2005) has suggested that under-achieving and under-served groups can potentially benefit from accountability reporting, when identified shortfalls come to light and are acted upon by their host organization. Conversely, the research literature gives cases where accountability practices have been conceived as punitive. For example, Webb (2005) describes how a model of educational accountability threatened to punish teachers through over-monitoring and intrusive surveillance.

Ryan (2005) contends that accountability mechanisms which require reaction to demands at the expense of pro-activity in improving teaching and learning are at fault. This author suggests that what is needed is an active engagement of a range of stakeholders such as teachers, learners, citizens and experts in a dialogue to create a self-monitoring community, active in constructing a workable and effective model of educational accountability. Ryan's reference to the inclusion of a variety of stakeholders in self-evaluation prompts consideration of the place of parents and pupils in mechanisms of school evaluation. Who should, and who should not should be included needs much further consideration and debate, especially in the light of the advantages and disadvantages of the place of pupil voice in improvement activities already explored in Chapter 5.

A case study undertaken in an international school in Hong Kong (Leung, 2005) suggests five conditions that can facilitate or hinder the implementation of school self-evaluation for the dual purposes of accountability and school development. These are framed as:

- a comprehensive school self-evaluation system which is an on-going cycle of planning, trying and evaluating;
- an appropriate set of implementation strategies, sow the seeds, let them talk, apply pressure and support;
- a dynamic pattern of shared values which is open to constant revisions and changes;
- a combination of leadership by the senior management team, distributed leadership and leadership by critical learning;
- a genuine belief in the talent of every single individual at the school.

This work suggests that leaders who foster collaboration and trust between staff, so that the opinions of others are listened to and valued, are likely to increase the success of self-evaluation mechanisms intended to encompass both improvement and accountability requirements. This is suggested because the work may offer insights into the efficacy of collaboration, trust and leadership distribution, perhaps as part of the characteristics of a learning community, that allow both the identification of strengths and the accompanying rectification of identified weaknesses.

Educational improvement and self-evaluation

Rogers and Badham (1992) identified two main purposes for the evaluation of performance: first, accountability to improve quality and second, development to improve quality. As far as self-evaluation itself is concerned, MacGilchrist (2000) offers the argument that at least three types of interrelated self-evaluation should be addressed if the dual purposes of improvement and accountability are to be achieved:

- macro self-evaluation – which focuses on the school as a whole and seeks to elucidate the extent to which the school is maximizing its overall effectiveness as a learning community.
- means-ends self-evaluation – which focuses on the extent to which schoolwide plans for improvement are impacting on the classroom and, in particular, on pupils' progress and achievements in classrooms.

- micro self-evaluation – which focuses not only on learning outcomes, but also on the quality of the learning taking place in the classroom.

Undertaking self-evaluation entails identifying the evaluation focus, deciding on the information needed, how it will be secured using what instruments, ensuring that the timing of information collection is appropriately placed and analysing the data to answer the questions posed, followed by action on the identified findings (see Herman and Winters, 1992). The need for valid and reliable data is important if the self-evaluation is to be credible and have the usefulness to serve its required purposes. Neil *et al.* (2001) suggest that self-evaluation requires a school structure and culture that will facilitate the gathering of data. Sources of important data must not be overlooked. For example, Demie (2003) shows how value-added research undertaken at local author-ity level can be used directly by heads and teachers in their efforts to raise standards in schools. McNamara and O'Hara (2005) caution that if self-evaluation is to become a basis for school improvement and a credible form of quality assurance and accounta-bility, then the data collected must ensure that both are achievable. Again, the focus for the evaluation and an understanding of what data is to be collected, by whom, and from where, so that it will be fit for purpose, will offer a challenge to those leaders, managers and teachers involved in its organization and operation. McNamara and O'Hara (2005) report on the rise in self-evaluation in Ireland and describe a new sys-tem of whole-school evaluation called Looking at Our Schools (LAOS). This frame-work requires schools to produce high-quality data on which to base judgements about quality and plans for improvement. However, research by McNamara and O'Hara (2006) showed that teachers in schools were finding undertaking systematic self-evaluative research difficult. This may represent a major barrier and suggests that teachers need training in how to better reflect, collect relevant data and self-evaluate.

Neil and Johnston (2003) list their own perspectives on issues crucial to the suc-cessful development of self-evaluation. These include:

- developing in-depth ownership of the self-evaluation, so that it becomes embed-ded in both planning and everyday activity;
- ensuring that self-evaluation and its purpose are made clear and are understood by all;
- ensuring that teachers' workloads are reviewed, so that time and energy are avail-able for self-evaluation activity;
- ensuring that there is a climate conducive to the development of the skills of analysis, reflection, communication and collaboration required for effective self-evaluation.

One of the earliest models of school self-evaluation in England was the GRIDS sys-tem (McMahon *et al.*, 1984). Many new models have developed over the past few years. For example in Holland, Hofman *et al.* (2005) report on the plethora of instruments available for school self-evaluation and have offered a new schedule aimed at facilitat-ing data collection, taking into account both school improvement and accountability requirements. MacBeath (1999) and MacBeath *et al.* (2000) have suggested a list of the key indicators to be addressed with respect to school self-evaluation and school improvement. These include: school climate; relationships; organization and communication; time and resources; recognition of achievement; equity; home–school links; support for teaching; classroom climate and support for learning. MacBeath *et al.* (2000) go on to highlight some of the main data collection methods likely to be used in school self-evaluations; these include interviews, questionnaires, observations, focus groups and documentary analysis. The methods and instruments employed reflect those used in other forms of research and need to embody credibility in their selection and use, as well as the desired utility as a basis for improvement activities. There is an assumption that staff in schools or their advisers are able to undertake evaluative research and that the sources of their data, whether documentary or human, are able to yield information that reflects as high a degree of validity and reliability as possible.

Wroe and Halsall (1999) advocate a self-critical community approach to self-evaluation for improvement, involving teachers investigating and reflecting on their own practices with the empowerment to modify these practices on the basis of their own professional judgement. However, engagement in critical reflection is not always easy; Humphreys and Susak (1999) point out that different workplace conditions can strongly influence opportunities to be reflective and that teachers need to be engaged enough in their work to want to reflect in the first place. It is also true that some individuals may not know how to be critically reflective and may need support to achieve this. Although self-evaluation is very likely to be supported by the school's adoption of the characteristics of a professional learning community as described in Chapter 5, these characteristics are unlikely to be well developed in all schools and in all departments. Visscher and Witziers (2004) found that some subject departments were some distance from the achievement of more professionally organized communities. Neil and Johnston (2003) suggest that the development of a culture of self-evaluation in schools is promoted when the leadership of the head and senior staff is transformational, when advice, guidance and support are available to the school when needed, and when schools have access to appropriate tools and methodologies for generating data.

Davies and Rudd (2001) report that an evaluation of self-evaluation involving 16 schools in England found the following positive outcomes for schools:

- a cultural dimension involving a positive impact on openness to exploring different methods of evaluating practice;
- a professional development dimension through dissemination of good practices;
- an organizational development opportunity as a basis for change;
- enhanced involvement with other stakeholders such as parents and governors who could provide feedback on the school;
- the acquisition of a critical friend in the form of a Local Education Authority (LEA) adviser or consultant who could facilitate the process.

The notion of the role of a critical friend has attracted interest in the UK and it has been suggested that the contribution of an external agent can be of value in offering both support and objectivity during self-evaluation (see MacBeath, 1999). As suggested by Davies and Rudd (2001), a critical friend may be a local authority adviser, a consultant or indeed some other individual with experience of school improvement and ideally experience of school self-evaluation. It would be highly beneficial to the process if the chosen critical friend is trusted within the school and is able to get to know all school stakeholders very well. Swaffield (2003) lists many of the ways in which a critical friend can help a school in the process of developing self-knowledge, and comments on the fact that because such a critical friend is external to the school they are likely to be better-placed to see things with a different view and ask difficult questions. Swaffield (2004) emphasizes that trust is a necessary condition for critical friendship, given the critical friend's potentially powerful position in supporting leadership and school improvement.

Swaffield and MacBeath (2005) describe how the new Ofsted framework for inspecting schools that came into operation in September 2003 strengthened inspectors' use of schools' own self-evaluation information to help them focus their own inspection. These authors review the intention in England to move school self-evaluation to a position where it is at the heart of the inspection. They describe the use of a school self-evaluation form (SEF) upon which data can be provided to the inspection team. This new relationship with schools was highlighted by Government Minister David Miliband in January 2004:

> There are three key aspects to a new relationship with schools. An accountability framework, which puts a premium on ensuring effective and ongoing self-evaluation in every school combined with more focused external inspection, linked closely to the improvement cycle of the school. A simplified school improvement process, where every school uses robust self-evaluation to drive improvement, informed by a single annual conversation with a school improvement partner to debate and advise on targets, priorities and support. And improved information and data management between schools, government bodies and parents with information collected once, used many times.
>
> (DfES, 2004b)

The new relationship adopted with schools appears to be located as one of the models of self-evaluation and external evaluation described by Alvik (1997), who identified three predominant models of self-evaluation and external evaluation:

- parallel: in which the two systems run side by side each other with their own criteria and protocols;
- sequential: in which external bodies follow on from the school's own evaluation and use that as the focus of their quality assurance system;
- cooperative: in which external agencies cooperate with schools to develop a common approach to evaluation.

The relationship seems to follow the 'sequential' model. As such it may reflect, depending upon particular viewpoints, either a far more trusting approach to bring forward an organization's potentially deeper knowledge of its own contextualized understanding of its strengths and areas for improvement, or alternatively a means to reduce the costs associated with more expensive external inspection.

In the following sections, Alvik's modelling will be used to further examine the place of self-evaluation in schools, further education and higher education institutions; the implications for leadership within those institutions will also be explored.

Self-evaluation and schools in the UK

In England and Wales, school inspections conducted by Ofsted have been supplemented by self-evaluation since 1996. Emphasizing accountability to stakeholders and the need to drive school improvement, a document produced by the Department for Education and Skills entitled *A New Relationship with Schools: improving performance through school self-evaluation* (DfES, 2004c) sets out the intended relationship between school self-evaluation and school improvement. This document suggests how to get the most out of self-evaluation and how to use the findings to plan for school improvement. It also discusses the relationship between school self-evaluation and external inspection provided by Ofsted:

> To get the greatest benefit from inspection, head teachers and governing bodies will need to ensure that their school has undertaken an objective evaluation of its performance, identified priorities for improvement and set achievable targets. Ofsted's SEF (self-evaluation form) provides schools with a means of capturing the findings of their self-evaluation.
>
> (DfES, 2004c: 3)

The document suggests that self-evaluation should not be undertaken solely for the purpose of inspection, and that schools should shape for themselves a self-evaluation process that is straightforward, doable and is integrated in existing routine management systems. It is suggested that schools should evaluate all they do, but this does not have to be done all at the same time. Schools are free to adopt any model which gives them the best insights into their improvement priorities. Six questions are posed:

* does the self-evaluation identify how well our school serves its learners?
* how does our school compare with the best comparable schools?
* is the self-evaluation integral to our key management systems?
* is our school's self-evaluation based on a good range of telling evidence?
* does our self-evaluation and planning involve key people in the school and seek the views of parents, learners and external advisers and agencies?
* does our self-evaluation lead to action to achieve the school's longer term goals for development?

The self-evaluation form (SEF) provided by Ofsted is intended to be a place to record and summarize the findings of the self-evaluation process. It is suggested that the school's leaders may find the questions in the SEF helpful in guiding their self-evaluation and that the SEF should be updated annually. Ofsted inspectors use the completed SEF to judge how well a school's senior staff and governors know the organization's strengths and areas for improvement. From 2009, draft self-evaluation forms have been made available online (http://www.ofsted.gov.uk) and require schools to provide information and details pertaining to:

- the context of the school;
- pupil outcomes;
- effectiveness of provision;
- effectiveness of leadership and management;
- effectiveness of early years foundation stage (if appropriate to the school);
- effectiveness of the sixth form (if appropriate to the school).

From September 2009, the 'Evaluation Schedule for Schools', provided by Ofsted, mirrors SEF items and shows what inspectors will report on.

Overall, the model adopted for UK schools appears 'sequential', with external inspection following on from the school's own evaluation. There are elements of the adoption of a 'cooperative' model, as indicated by the greater alignment of the self-evaluation form and the Evaluation Schedule for schools. As mentioned previously, schools are left to choose the actual mechanisms of self-evaluation for themselves; however the provision of a common SEF recording mechanism and its reflection in the Ofsted Evaluation Schedule for schools suggests standardization, not only for inspectors, but also across the system with respect to the quality of self-evaluation. A more 'cooperative' approach could be seen as offering greater regard for teacher professionalism, acknowledgement of local contextual issues and the provision of some external inspection pressure if difficult decisions need to be made. Importantly, schools and teachers need to be able to see and believe in the development possibilities that can emerge from self-evaluation, or their efforts in data collection will be seen as lacking purpose and greedy of time that could be used elsewhere in the school. As the 'new relationship' develops it will become clearer how it is perceived within schools and how useful it is in effecting improvement.

Self-evaluation and further education

In England, the post-compulsory education and training sector is now referred to as the Learning and Skills sector. The New Labour government, via the Learning and Skills Act of July 2000, created a Learning and Skills Council (LSC) which is presently the planning and funding body for the post-compulsory sector, including adult and community learning and school sixth forms. The Learning and Skills Act also brought into existence the Adult Learning Inspectorate (ALI), which shares inspection responsibility in the further education sector with Ofsted, the latter being primarily responsible for provision for younger learners. Both were required to work within a *Common Inspection Framework* (ALI/Ofsted, 2005). The inspectorates concern themselves with quality of provision and the LSC monitors the performance of providers and offers support post-inspection. A group of Local Learning and Skills Councils (LLSCs) have also attempted to engage themselves with monitoring quality assurance through requests to local providers for data such as achievement and retention rates. Although improvement is firmly on the college sector agenda, overall, the sector has been thought to have a system leaning towards quality assurance and accountability rather than improvement of learning. There is evidence that this balance is changing.

The *Common Inspection Framework for Further Education and Skills* in 2009 is very much concerned with overall organizational effectiveness and capacity to improve. The framework specifically seeks information about the outcomes of learners, the quality of provision and the effectiveness of organizational leadership and management.

Much greater reliance on self-assessment is becoming a feature of inspection, although some concern remains that providers may shy away from admitting faults due to their place in a competitive contract environment. The *Common Inspection Framework* is used by colleges as a basis for their annual self-assessment activities. In order to ensure that learners' needs are met, and areas for improvement are identified, colleges ask themselves:

- how well do learners achieve?
- how effective are teaching, training and learning?
- how well are learners guided and supported?
- how effective are leadership and management in raising achievement and supporting all learners?

The internal assessments undertaken by colleges are then used by Ofsted to inform the scope of their Annual Assessment Visit and by the LSC to assess risks, inform an annual Provider Review, and inform annual planning and allocation of funding. Like that for schools, overall the model adopted on behalf of the UK college sector appears 'sequential' with the beginnings of 'cooperation' given the greater reliance on self-evaluation. Evaluation within the sector is working to balance accountability with an emphasis on leadership for learning and the improvement of learner outcomes and in this respect more closely mirrors the relationship of internal and external evaluation prevalent in the schools sector.

Self-evaluation and higher education

Quality assessment has become a feature of the landscape in higher education. In the mid-1990s Yorke (1995) drew attention to the need for higher education institutions (HEIs) to be self-critical of the quality of their academic programmes. At a time when Total Quality Management (TQM) was viewed as an essential approach to ensure the quality of many organizations in the public and private sectors, notions of TQM and re-engineering began to find some favour as self-regulatory mechanisms in some schools, colleges and HEIs. Any associated 'quality marks' were seen as helpful marketing tools in convincing the new 'market-led' consumers of education to choose one institution over another. However many HEIs ignored the TQM movement, despite the demands for quality assurance procedures, response to client needs and enhanced outputs being made by governments at that time (see Kells, 1995).

In the under-researched higher education sector many questions remain. What constitutes quality in higher education? Are there different quality priorities in research-led and in teaching-led universities? Institutions would no doubt contend that evaluations were very much concerned with improvement and accountability, as in the schools and further education sectors. In Australia, Carmichael *et al.* (2001) have surveyed the development of various approaches to quality that are essentially learning-centred and suggest a strong case for student learning to be placed at the heart of quality systems in higher education. In Holland, Tigelaar *et al.* (2004) have offered insights into the development and validation of a framework for teaching competencies in higher education. In this study, teaching competencies in student-centred higher education are defined as an integrated set of personal characteristics, knowledge, skills and attitudes that are needed for effective performance in various teaching contexts. Seven domains are identified:

- person as a teacher;
- expert on content knowledge;
- facilitator of learning: Developer;
- facilitator of learning: Counsellor;
- facilitator of learning: Evaluator;
- facilitator of learning: Organizer;
- facilitator of learning: Scholar/lifelong learner.

In the UK, the external evaluation mechanisms already seen in the schools and further education sectors have found a foothold in the higher education sector. The quality of continuing professional development provision for teachers has received attention from HMI/Ofsted inspection with attendant public reporting of outcomes. Initial teacher training (ITT) programmes receive regular inspection visits from Ofsted and public reporting can have an impact upon present and potential students and funding bodies. Reporting can also lead to the expansion or reduction of places and also bring about course closure. The New Labour government emphasized a relationship between learning and economic growth and advocated increased student numbers, a culture of improvement and high teaching quality in higher education. As already mentioned in this text, the introduction of quality assurance schemes has been met with a mixed reception in higher education. The Quality Assurance Agency's (QAA) subject review, for example, consisting of a self-assessment document and an external inspection, has raised some staff suspicion and defensiveness (Gosling, 2000). As introduced in Chapter 2 the QAA checks how UK universities maintain their own academic standards and quality. They report on how universities meet their responsibilities, identify good practice and make recommendations for improvement. The QAA publishes guidelines to help UK universities and colleges develop systems to ensure that all students have the best learning experience. Reviews are carried out using a variety of methods, depending on the constituent UK country and the type of institution. For example, in England and Northern Ireland, institutional audit is the review process adopted for higher education organizations. In England, a collaborative provision audit looks at how institutions with degree-awarding powers ensure the standards of their awards when these awards are delivered at other partner institutions. Integrated quality enhancement review, however, is the method used for higher education delivered in colleges of further education. The preparation of a self-evaluation document by the higher education organization to be reviewed is integral to the process of review. For example, in an integrated quality and enhancement review undertaken in England, the purpose of the self-evaluation is to report the responsibilities which the college has within the area of student assessment and to reflect upon and evaluate the effectiveness of the processes and procedures it uses in the area of student assessment.

In addition to self-evaluation for QAA audit, internal self-evaluation mechanisms linked to institutional quality frameworks are now commonplace in higher education and offer improvement insights, as well as providing accountability information to a range of interested internal and external stakeholders. Institutional quality frameworks are likely to seek data collection, reflection and improvement planning with respect to individual programmes as well as for larger groupings such as departments and schools. At a programme level, student evaluation forms are routinely collected at the end of units of teaching. These forms typically include feedback from students concerning the quality of teaching, resources, quality of feedback and assessment and support provided. Such internal evaluations are used in annual monitoring procedures for these individual programmes, leading to the production of an action plan intended to frame any necessary improvement actions. There is concern that student evaluation forms may reveal whether students 'liked' the unit of teaching rather than giving an objective view of 'quality'. Peer observation of teaching by lecturing staff has become a feature of HEI practice during the last decade and has become integral to quality reviews (Shortland, 2004). This generally involves peers observing each other's teaching and offering feedback to facilitate reflection and the sharing of good practice.

Overall, the model of self-evaluation prevalent within the UK higher education sector appears to have moved from former 'parallelism' to a much greater degree of 'sequentialism' in the face of increased frequency of external evaluation mechanisms. Indeed, within the authors' own experience, QAA auditors are usually keen to speak to members of university staff to gain insights and explanations of procedures and systems so that better-informed judgements can be made.

Conclusion

This chapter has attempted to offer insights into self-evaluation as a mechanism firmly linked to the requirements of improvement and accountability within the schools, further education and higher education sectors. A theme common to all three sectors is a desire to improve, serve the needs of stakeholders well and raise outcomes for learners. The balance between self-evaluation and external evaluation shows some commonality between these sectors, with firm moves in recent years to more sequential approaches where self-evaluation as part of internal quality assurance is used in offering focus to audits undertaken by external bodies. A question emerges as to who should be involved in offering information for internal self-evaluation. Should all stakeholders, including learners themselves, have a voice? Notwithstanding the inescapable influences of government policy and sector and organizational differences, a conclusion may be drawn that the more evaluation is perceived to be aimed at accountability and is seen as alienating and threatening to staff, the less likely it is that evaluation will be useful to organizational improvement. If this is so, then leadership and management have an important role in enabling teachers to seek and attain the improvement benefits that can emerge from self-evaluation processes. Given rigour, credibility and utility then self-evaluation can constitute an important basis for improvement effort. However, support for the self-evaluating teacher may well be needed, as not all individuals are able to reflect critically and be reflexive about their actions so that new and improved practices may emerge. Indeed, self-evaluation demands, in any institution, that there are individuals with skill in the collection and analysis of data from a variety of sources. Although there are many available frameworks to offer help and guidance, inexperience may be a barrier to depth and progress in some instances. Although not explored within the confines of this chapter, it is established that self-evaluation on the part of students can help improve the quality of their work and could be further encouraged by organizational leaders and managers seeking to raise the outcomes of learners. For example, Hinett and Weeden (2000) showed that both peer assessment and self-assessment could help trainee teachers to develop their qualitative judgements, improve confidence, enhance motivation to learn and increase ownership of subject content. Also a study of high-school students (McDonald and Boud, 2003) concluded that those students trained by their teachers to undertake self-assessment showed positive impact upon their performance overall and in each curriculum area. It is suggested that leaders should not neglect the potential of self-evaluation at all levels within their organization.

9 Leadership and external inspection

Introduction

This chapter will examine key issues in the external inspection of educational organizations. In particular, developments in the Ofsted inspection framework in the UK will be reviewed and key lessons for leaders will be drawn out. The chapter will examine:

- schools and their relationship with their environment;
- partnerships for learning, especially in working with parents;
- external accountability and Ofsted inspection;
- an illustration of approaches to inspection;
- the essence of successful accountability.

We conclude by suggesting that subject leaders need to keep at the forefront of their minds that their work on accountability has both a professional and moral dimension and we emphasize the importance of recent developments in the theory of leadership such as notions of distributed leadership.

Schools and their relationship with their environment

One of the most important tasks for subject leaders is to ensure that the quality of teaching and learning is constantly monitored, with clear signs of progress and an upward trend of achievement for *all* pupils (Brundrett and Terrell, 2004). This monitoring will key into the school improvement cycles outlined in the last chapter, but it serves a further function which is to inform other stakeholders about the progress of the subject and, ultimately, of the school. Moreover, much of the literature on organizational theory reflects an increasing concern for the 'environment' that surrounds institutions. The open systems view goes so far as to suggest that organizations will always have some form of boundaries, but that these are subject to being spanned, crossed or otherwise traversed in some manner. These ideas are especially important in the context of schools since schools have so many groups of people who they wish to serve and to please. For this reason one interesting notion that is especially relevant to schools is the concept of *permeability*, examined in some detail earlier in this text, by which we mean the ability for both egress and ingress of information, ideas, people and products. Since schools are set within a stakeholder community that includes not only staff and pupils but also parents, local and national authorities and society as a whole, schools are some of the most permeable organizations of all (Goldring, 1997: 290). It is, however, something of a bitter irony that this increasing need to develop links with the community comes at a time when schools are increasingly concerned about security in a way that often leads to the construction of physical barriers to access. In this context it is ever more important that the aims and goals and day-to-day activities of the organization are communicated effectively both within and beyond the actual 'edges' of the school as a physical entity.

The role of subject leader within these overlapping communication structures and groupings is to occupy a middle management position within the school's hierarchical structure which provides a 'layer' of management between the senior management team and those at the chalk face (Fleming and Amesbury, 2001: 2). Typically, in a traditional management model in secondary schools, subject leaders are positioned between classroom teachers and the head and senior management team. No such layer exists in most primary schools, although larger primaries and middle schools may employ such staffing structures and even smaller primaries may have co-ordinators (or otherwise designated staff) who take a leading role in managing infant and junior departments. Such staff play a key role in helping to move a school forward in terms of its improvement plans, strategic development, overall goals and mission statement. They are also expected to ensure the smooth day-to-day running of the school's business and to monitor the progress of pupils and those staff within their department or subject team.

Internally, subject leaders are accountable upwards to the head and senior management team and downwards to the teachers in their subject teams and the pupils they teach. They are also accountable to school governors, parents and less directly to education policy-makers and politicians. As has already been mentioned in this text, these accountability groupings are sometimes referred to as *stakeholders*, a term which is often used loosely to categorize 'all those who have a legitimate interest in the continuing effectiveness and success of an institution' (Waring, 1999: 180, see also Chapters 6 and 7). However, the term could be equally well applied to pupils, departmental staff and key personnel higher up the chain of command, all of whom are internal to the institution and each of whom have a legitimate interest in the effectiveness and success of an institution. A more helpful grouping recognizes that there are different interests and value systems depending on whether you are a pupil, a parent or a politician. For example, Becher *et al.* (1979) recognize that a teacher has three kinds of accountability: moral (to pupils and parents as clients); professional (to one's colleagues) and contractual (to the school governing body and political masters). As already established in this text, an emerging further type is market accountability, which is intended to foster client choice of the institution they might attend. These sets of relationships serve a variety of functions but two are of especial relevance to this chapter:

- partnerships for learning – we argue that schools should be learning organizations and this can only become the case if parents and other carers are involved in the educational enterprise.

- accountability – schools must, by law, be accountable for their actions and performance as measured by the Ofsted inspection regime and performance indicators such as examination and assessment results.

Partnerships for learning – working with parents

Attitudes to parents have changed dramatically over the professional life of the last generation of teachers. It was once the case that the prevailing view of teachers and heads was that parents were firmly encouraged to stay outside the school gates – leaving the process of education to teachers who acted as autonomous professionals in their own classrooms. It might be too dramatic to say that the gates have been thrown open in recent years (although that is true in some schools) but it is certainly true that there has been a gradual and developing belief that parents should be encouraged to be intimately involved in their child's education, both at home and in school. This new attitude has, in part, been thrust upon schools because of the more market-driven ideology of education, exemplified in the Education Acts of 1988 and 1992, which gave parents the opportunity to choose which school they sent their child to. To some extent such choice is actually illusory, since in the most popular schools there are often insufficient places to take the number of children whose parents would like them to attend. Nonetheless the overall impact of the removal of fixed catchment areas has been that school leaders have had to think very carefully about whether or not they are pleasing both pupils and parents, in a way which would not have been the case in earlier periods.

The imperative to involve parents has increased as both governmental initiatives and educational research have increasingly stressed the role of parents in enhancing learning. Since 1994 Ofsted have investigated the level of involvement of parents in school life and their attitude to their children's schools. The White Paper *Excellence in Schools* (DfEE, 1997) stressed the importance of parents as co-educators with teachers and the pupils themselves. These notions about parental involvement in learning had initial impact, especially in the area of literacy, since a number of studies have shown the importance of the family in creating a home environment that would support children's learning in school and beyond (see Hannon, 2000). Such ideas began to impact on national policy in the late 1990s when the Literacy Task Force (1997: 32) stated that: 'Parents have a vital role in supporting and encouraging children's learning, perhaps most of all in helping that child to read'. The subsequent National Literacy Strategy and Numeracy Strategy incorporated parental engagement as a central element of their approach and the overall National Primary Strategy, embodied in *Excellence and Enjoyment* (DfES, 2003c: 47) states that: 'partnership with parents is critical to helping children to achieve as well as they possibly can'.

The National Strategy also symbolizes a move beyond links with parents to a broader agenda of 'joined up thinking' which seeks to integrate the whole community into the education of children. The strategy suggests that detailed parental involvement strategies should be developed locally, so that they really meet local needs and goes on to state that support should be coordinated through local preventative strategies, which bring together all those agencies responsible for services for children, young people and families (DfES, 2003c: 48–49). Taking this as the starting point, the National Strategy suggests that parental engagement should:

- build on Sure Start and other Early Years programmes, particularly as children transfer from Early Years settings to school, so that it is clear to parents that they still have an important role;
- support parents in helping their children learn – through family learning projects and also support for parenting skills;
- take a multi-agency approach to supporting parents in engaging with their children's learning;
- make it clear that parents have responsibilities too.

(DfES, 2003c: 49–50)

This commitment to communities of learning is underpinned by the notion of 'extended schools', introduced in Chapter 7, which support standards because, with more opportunities for out-of-hours learning, they take a wider approach to supporting children's learning, and help build schools into the fabric of the local community by offering easy access to a range of educational and other services for children, families and other members of the community. The government's aim is that, over time, all schools will provide at least some of these services, and some schools will go further and offer a comprehensive range of activities and support. It is envisaged that each full service school will offer a prescribed core of childcare, study support, family and lifelong learning, health and social care, parenting support, sports and arts facilities, and ICT access.

The notion of working with parents is, however, more complex than the exhortations for involvement might suggest. At the most pragmatic and practical level parents may well be disinclined to be involved in their children's schools, perhaps because of their own experiences of education (Merchant and March, 1998; Osler *et al.*, 2000). The concept of extended schools is laudable, but presents ever more challenges to the leadership of schools, at all levels, at a time when multiple innovations are already problematic and time-consuming. Schools need to ensure that they ask key questions in order to facilitate this movement towards wider engagement. Edwards and Waring (1999) suggest a number of implications for practitioners when seeking to involve parents based around a series of questions including:

- does your home–school policy have a clear rationale for parental involvement?
- is your rationale for parental involvement all about school-led demands?
- do you have a way of finding out what parents think about their child, their child's education and what they view as important?
- what does the school ask parents to do with children? Does this build on what parents know and can do?
- does the school know if its strategies for parental involvement contribute to increased learning?
- are the tasks parents are asked to do equally accessible for all parents?
- do the teachers have an opportunity to find out what parents can contribute and how they see their children's schooling?
- are parent workshops planned with the needs of the parents in mind?

Overall, the enhanced interest in parental and wider community engagement in education is to be applauded since it links with developing research findings about the nature of learning. The increasing engagement of governmental bodies in such initiatives is also to be welcomed since it provides impetus and focus for such initiatives but subject leaders, who will play a key role in developing such relationships, must be aware of the inherent challenges that they face in integrating parents and the wider community into networks of support.

External accountability and Ofsted inspection

The 1988 Education Reform Act replaced the principles of universalism and social equality enshrined in the 1944 Act with the ideology of the market via individualism, public choice and accountability. Indeed it can be argued that accountability is the concomitant of enabling schools to become market-driven and self-managing. Decentralization has been viewed as a key way to improve efficiency, not only in schools but across all organizations. Yet central government must continue to monitor what goes on in schools in order to ensure that they are improving and, in turn, to be accountable to their electorate. Accountability can thus be regarded as a counterpart of the greater freedom at institutional level (Anderson, 2005: 75).

The varying forms of accountability may be seen as a continuum from local, professionally dominated systems to the kind of externally driven systems which appear to have dominated the early Ofsted model. Scott (1999) draws on the work of Halstead and considers five models of accountability, one of which, *the evaluative state model* (Scott, 1999), was particularly applicable to state primary and secondary schools until a re-evaluation of the Ofsted framework in the late 1990s. Within this model, the state gives over the precise implementation of policy to semi-independent bodies such as Ofsted which, whilst accountable to government ministers, override existing forms of accountability such as LEA-school relations (Duncan, 2003). In this model, the inspection process itself becomes the means by which schools comply with government policy (Scott, 1999: 27). With its regular cycle of inspections and severe sanctions for failing and under-performing schools, Ofsted was granted significant powers to compel schools to conform to government prescriptions on its behalf. Despite the externality and apparent rigour and clarity of this system Scott claimed that 'systems of accountability . . . can never be imposed absolutely. There is, in other words, space within any imposed model for local initiative' (Scott, 1999: 30). Thus school managers were undoubtedly proactive in seeking to influence the accountability structures by finding ways of managing and controlling the inspection process in ways which better served the interests of school staff, parents and pupils. Such schools have learned to use external accountability systems to their advantage as well as to improve and develop themselves.

Nonetheless, the Ofsted model of external scrutiny of schools has been subject to a sustained critique since its inception in the early 1990s. The regime has been criticized both with regard to its practical efficacy in raising standards of achievement and, more conceptually, for its flawed and sometimes inimical attitudes to efficiency and effectiveness. Early follow-up studies revealed that few school development plans rooted in inspection findings actually followed through on the issues identified in the inspection process, despite the fact that most staff accepted the issues identified needed to be addressed (Gray and Wilcox, 1995; Brundrett and Silcock, 2002: 64). Moreover, it has been suggested that the Ofsted school-inspection regime, especially as it existed in its first iteration, conflated the two concepts of efficiency and effectiveness without unpacking the complex interrelationships usually existing between them (Fielding, 1997: 11), in that schools can be effective but profoundly inefficient if they 'add value' to student experience at unacceptable cost. Equally, schools can be efficient but ineffective if they arrange schooling at minimal cost but fail to educate students. One must question the nature of a school's efficiency if it leads to burgeoning workloads and surveillance for and of teachers (Ball, 1990). As Fielding points out (1997: 12), any recognition of the 'non-neutral' status of efficiency begs the question as to whose interests shape the nature and process of work.

Market-led visions of schooling exclude any exploration of the potentially problematic nature of the curriculum. School work is usually seen as dealing with a fixed, immutable body of knowledge, with any alterations justified according to the dominant paradigm of increased effectiveness (Brundrett and Silcock, 2002: 225). It is, however, important to remember no particular model of accountability is static or immutable since systems of accountability are value-laden and can change, depending on the particular historical and political circumstances of the time (Duncan, 2003). The latter part of the 1990s saw a subtle shift in the relationship between Ofsted and the schools that they inspected from a hard-edged external system to a more inclusive set of practices which increasingly took account of the views of the school's leadership team.

This more recent form of inspection is more contingent on school self-evaluation as depicted in Chapter 8, a fact that adds further weight to arguments in favour of democratic or co-constructive teaching that are discussed in Chapter 10. The point to stress is that co-constructive teaching depends on ongoing critical self-evaluation: generalizing from ongoing particular circumstances to gain a picture of any one school's achievements should be a fairly straightforward business (Brundrett and Silcock, 2002: 177). This revised approach can be illustrated by reference to a school inspection framework as embodied in *Inspecting Schools: Framework for Inspecting Schools* (Ofsted, 2003b: 3) which outlines key principles:

- inspection acts in the interests of children, young people and adult learners and, where relevant, their parents, to encourage high-quality provision that meets diverse needs and promotes equality;
- inspection is evaluative and diagnostic, assessing quality and compliance, and providing a clear basis for improvement;
- the purpose of inspection and the procedures to be used are communicated clearly to those involved;
- inspection invites and takes account of any self-evaluation by those inspected;
- inspection informs those responsible for taking decisions about provision;
- inspection is carried out by those who have sufficient and relevant professional expertise and training;

- evidence is recorded and is of sufficient range and quality to secure and justify judgements;
- judgements are based on systematic evaluation requirements and criteria, are reached corporately where more than one inspector is involved, and reflect a common understanding in Ofsted about quality;
- effectiveness is central to judging the quality of provision and processes;
- inspection includes clear and helpful oral feedback and leads to written reporting that evaluates performance and quality, and identifies strengths and areas for improvement;
- the work of all inspectors reflects Ofsted's stated values and its code of conduct;
- quality assurance is built into all inspection activities to ensure that these principles are met and inspection is improved.

In law, it was established that inspections must report on:

- the educational standards achieved in the school;
- the quality of the education provided by the school;
- the quality of leadership and management, including whether the financial resources made available to the school are managed efficiently;
- the spiritual, moral, social and cultural development of pupils at the school.

In the illustrative example provided, the *Evaluation Schedule* in Part C of the *Framework* covers these four requirements by requiring inspectors to evaluate the following aspects of the school's work:

- standards achieved;
- pupils' attitudes, values and personal development;
- teaching and learning;
- the quality of the curriculum;
- the care, guidance and support of pupils;
- partnerships with parents, other schools and the community;
- leadership and management;
- the areas of learning, subjects and courses of the curriculum; and
- other matters that HMCI may specify.

Inspection helps the school by providing an overall judgement on the effectiveness of the school and identifying its strengths and weaknesses and the most important points for improvement.

Inspection and self-evaluation illustrated

Schools have a range of internal processes for monitoring their own performance and evaluating the effectiveness of their work in raising achievement. Such monitoring and evaluation should contribute, directly or indirectly, to periodic updating of the school improvement plan, which maps the priorities for action and sets out programmes for implementing them. Inspection takes account of or contributes to these processes in two ways.

A brief self-evaluation report prepared by the school helps to focus inspection effort where it matters most and to respond to any specific issues that the inspection can usefully include. The school's summary of its self-evaluation is used as the basis for discussion between the lead inspector and the headteacher and, where possible, governors of the school, when the inspection is being planned. Second, the quality and use made of school self-evaluation is a good indication of the calibre of management. Evidence of how effectively schools undertake self-evaluation and the use they make of it helps inspectors to evaluate the quality of management in the school and the capacity of the school to improve.

Ofsted introduced new arrangements for the inspection of state-maintained schools from late 2009. Schools are now provided with a new on-line self-evaluation form which seeks to secure information from schools concerning how well pupils are doing, how effective the provision is and the levels of effectiveness of leadership and management within the school. Sections also pursue information concerning early years and the sixth form should these be present within the school. The following text refers to current arrangements and is presented in order to illustrate internal evaluation as part of school inspection.

In order to promote the use of self-evaluation, a self-evaluation report (Form S4) is completed by the school before inspection, and is constructed so as to match the Evaluation Schedule used by inspectors. Many schools use the Evaluation Schedule as the basis for their internal evaluation processes (see Table 9.1). The lead inspector must allow sufficient time, both in the school before the inspection and in preparation,

Table 9.1 An illustrative example of an internal Evaluation Schedule used in Ofsted inspection

---

Evaluation Schedule: Contents

Effectiveness of the school

1. How successful is the school?
2. What should the school do to improve?

Standards achieved by pupils

3.1 How high are standards achieved in the areas of learning, subjects and courses of the curriculum?
3.2 How well are pupils' attitudes, values and other personal qualities developed?

Quality of education provided by the school

4. How effective are teaching and learning?
5. How well does the curriculum meet pupils' needs?
6. How well are pupils cared for, guided and supported?
7. How well does the school work in partnership with parents, other schools and the community?

Leadership and management of the school

8. How well is the school led and managed?
9. How good is the quality of education in areas of learning, subjects and courses?
10. What is the quality of other specified features?

---

to analyse and interpret the school's performance, identify issues and themes, and design and plan the inspection so that it will reflect the essence of the school. This process is intended to be thorough and consultative.

Ofsted has also published the following ten-point checklist that schools can use to evaluate their own commitment to Education for Sustainable Development (taken from: Ofsted, *Taking the first step forward . . . towards an education for sustainable development*, Annex C, 2003).

1. Could the school promote a culture and ethos which values the development, knowledge, attitudes and skills in pupils to enable them to participate individually and collectively to improve the quality of life in a sustainable way?
2. Has the school produced a policy statement for ESD which sets out the aims, priorities and targets for promoting ESD as a whole-school initiative, and identified strategies to promote and raise the profile of ESD within the school and the wider school community? Has it co-ordinated and monitored ESD initiatives and activities throughout the school to ensure a consistency of approach?
3. Is there a programme of staff development in place to raise awareness of ESD and develop teachers' competency and skills?
4. Have subject leaders identified opportunities within their schemes of work to enable ESD to be delivered and reinforced through the curriculum? Does the teaching approach promote active learning to develop pupils' understanding of sustainable development?
5. Does the school develop active and responsible citizenship and stewardship through pupils' involvement in active decision-making through a school council or eco-committee?
6. What links has the school established to support and develop a global and international dimension within the curriculum?
7. How does the school involve, and make use of, the wider school community to enrich learning and pupils' personal and social development including the effective use of business, local authorities, non-government organizations and community groups to support their work in developing the sustainable agenda?
8. In what ways does the school respect and value diversity?
9. In what active ways is the school involved in improving performance against sustainability indicators, including waste management, fair trade and a green purchasing policy?
10. Has the school embarked on, or maintained, a programme of ground development and improvement to support learning, promote stewardship and improve the quality of life?

(Ofsted, 2003a: 24)

Whatever demands are made upon subject teams with respect to accountability, the central focus must remain firmly on teaching and learning since this is the key to successful curriculum teams. However, there is now a new emphasis on the importance of all schools becoming inclusive schools. Since 2001, Ofsted school inspectors have received additional training to ensure that procedures for monitoring and inspecting entitlement for all pupils are tightened up. This not only means that there need to be robust systems in place to ensure that pupils with special educational needs have full access to the curriculum, but that the progress and well-being of pupils are not impeded or negatively affected by incidents of bullying and racism. This matters as much for the particular subject as it does for the school as a whole. Indeed, there is an important reference in the *National Standards for Subject Leadership* (TTA, 1998) which mentions the need for high expectations and success with pupils with special educational needs and linguistic needs as well as the requirement to ensure that teachers of the subject know how to recognize and deal with racial stereotyping.

The essence of successful accountability

What schools are facing today is part of the new culture of accountability, which is affecting most of the public sector. It demands increasing amounts of information, comparative data and target-setting without necessarily helping professionals to account for their practices and achievement in ways which parents, pupils and school governors might find interesting and helpful. One of the things which successful schools have done in recent years is to learn to control and manage accountability in ways which serve the interests of teachers, pupils and parents as well as the school community as a whole. It therefore matters that teacher managers do not blindly acquiesce to its prescriptions as though they were mere technicians. Their professional knowledge, experience and wisdom needs to inform every stage of the process because this is an important source of informed 'truth' which makes accountability of any kind make sense. Following on from this, one of the key requirements of subject leaders is to adopt an attitude and mind set which ensures that they control the process without letting it control them. Whatever paper systems and planning formats are used, certain fundamental principles should remain sacrosanct and these essentially concern the pupils, staff, parents and the school as a whole. The point of any accountability system must be to tell the truth, simply, clearly and in an open and transparent way (Brundrett and Terrell, 2004). This means that pupils are taught well, know what they need to do in order to improve, are prepared well for examinations and are enthusiastic about the subject. It means that parents are well informed about their children's achievements; know what is being done to help them if they are having difficulties and how they can support what the school is doing. As far as the subject team or department is concerned, it means ensuring that everyone works together as a team, knows and understands the broad and smaller picture in terms of the subject's development and has a clear sense of direction. Moreover, each individual's effort is recognized and valued and the team is kept up-to-date and fully informed of changes and new external initiatives. This collective endeavour needs then to be carefully aligned with the school's aims and mission statement so that policy is translated into practice through 'a logical progression from policy formulation to policy implementation within the planning hierarchy' (Giles, 1997).

Conclusion

Central government in the UK monitors schools in order to ensure that they are effective and improving and, in turn, central government offers account to its electorate. Giving account via inspection processes places demands upon school senior leaders, subject leaders and other school staff. The demands made upon subject teams with respect to accountability must not detract from their central focus on the quality of teaching and learning provided. In conclusion, subject leaders need to keep at the forefront of their minds that their work in accountability has both a professional and moral dimension. An ability to handle bureaucracy and keep up-to-date with paper work is clearly important but of far greater significance is their ability to engage teachers, pupils and parents in the accounting process in ways which demonstrate trust and belief in their staff and students. The way may then be open for them to work towards their version of intelligent accountability (Brundrett and Terrell, 2004).

To be successful at accountability, subject leaders need to be strong on paper systems and to be able to produce spreadsheets and data sources as a matter of course. If manageable, user-friendly ways of dealing with the paper work can be found, it then becomes easier to focus on the more important aspects of the task. These include being proactive and ahead of the game so that new initiatives and demands can be anticipated without becoming yet another burden. New developments and improvements needed for the subject need to be made with an eye on the strategy, mission, aims and vision of the whole school. Most important of all is the team itself which needs to feel a collective ownership of the vision and the direction of the educational organization or department. This means that individual members of the team need to be given specific areas of responsibility which draw upon their respective strengths and qualities. The concept of *distributed leadership* is an important concept in the more recent literature on schools facing challenging contexts (see especially, Harris, 2003 and Gray and Wilcox, 1995). Quite simply, this means that responsibility is devolved throughout the schools so that there are many rather than a few leaders. The power of praise, involving others in decision-making and giving professional autonomy to individual teachers are examples of some of its most effective strategies. This approach to leadership can be equally well applied to the subject team.

10 The future of quality and accountability in education

Introduction

In this, the final chapter of this book, we return to some of the themes introduced in preceding chapters. We commence by acknowledging, once again, that the twin terms 'quality' and 'accountability' are especially problematic in the field of education but relate to topics that cannot be avoided within education systems as they are now constructed. We will go on to examine:

*   continuing problems of what we mean by quality in education;
*   new frameworks for quality in education;
*   new frameworks for inspection and evaluation: balancing external and internal quality and accountability processes;
*   using students to enhance quality;
*   balancing quality and accountability with autonomy.

We conclude by noting an increasing commitment to self-regulation and the general movement in leadership towards system-wide approaches to the management of educational institutions.

The continuing problem of what we mean by quality in education

Notions of quality and accountability are certain to remain problematic at all phases in the field of education. Over 25 years ago, at a time of dramatic expansion in higher education in the UK, Ball pointed out the extreme difficulties in defining what we mean by quality in the tertiary sector:

> 'Quality in education' is a subject extraordinarily difficult to come to grips with, and full of pitfalls. There is no single final answer to the quality question and we should not look for it. But the issue cannot be avoided.
>
> (Ball, 1985: 96)

Such comments could apply equally to school education and time has done little to make them less pertinent or accurate. Quality and accountability are beset with problems, whether applied to education or the wider business sector, since one can always ask questions such as: Who defines what is meant by quality? Who is the organization accountable to? Will strategies to enhance quality and accountability impinge on the rights of workers? Such questions are especially problematic in education, where the multiplicity of stakeholders in schools, colleges and higher education settings means that there may be multiple and overlapping demands on such organizations. For instance it is quite possible that parents may take one, entirely justifiable, view of what kind of curriculum and teaching and learning strategies should be employed, pupils and students may take another and government agencies may have yet another view. This is to say nothing of the many other groups who have a legitimate interest in how schools and other educational organizations are run such as governors, Local Authorities, the local community, regional government agencies, local businesses and the wider public. We have noted earlier that schools, in particular, are highly permeable organizations and this seems unlikely to change. Leaders in education are required to balance these sometimes competing demands whilst at the same time fulfilling statutory responsibilities placed upon them.

New frameworks for quality in education

One of the most significant central initiatives in the UK has been the *Every Child Matters* agenda (TSO, 2004), in which the UK government has emphasized an increasingly integrative approach to enhancing quality which links all aspects of child services, including schools, social and health services and other functions of local authorities such as library services. In rising to the challenge of what is envisioned to be 'creating a consistently excellent system' (TSO, 2007: 98), it is necessary that all schools reach the level where emphasis is placed on a local accountability system focused on promoting continuing improvement in the classroom. Within this initiative, the stated intention is to act decisively to:

- *eradicate failure*, addressing the underperformance that is often a prelude to failure, and not tolerate failure where it occurs;
- *challenge complacency*, and in doing so work to eliminate wide variations within a school – where average whole-school performance masks some very poor
  standards in some areas; and
- *incentivize every school to improve*, driving satisfactory and good schools to become outstanding organizations and promoting a culture of ambition across the sector.

(TSO, 2007: 99)

In order to achieve these goals it is envisaged that parents will become partners in learning (TSO, 2007: 57–59) and a much greater emphasis will be placed on personalization in learning participation. It is claimed that the hallmarks of these ambitious objectives will include challenging personal targets, rapid intervention to keep pupils on trajectory, and vigorous assessment to check and maintain progress. In order to achieve these goals there is a continued emphasis on leadership skills in schools and a series of challenging goals have been established that include making teaching an all-Master's level profession and a continued emphasis on in-service leadership training (TSO, 2007: 83).

These aims place stress on system-wide reform and development and mirror international perspectives on enhancing quality in education. Many of the most important developments in this field derive from the US experience, so an examination of recent developments in that nation may foreshadow wider application. For instance, we may note that the American Society for Quality (ASQ) (2008) argues that the US education system needs to deliver the knowledge and skills that students need, and to respond as those needs change, and suggests that quality tools and processes can help. They suggest that methods are needed to judge the performance of processes within the system by establishing accountability processes that ensure a systematic method of assuring stakeholders (educators, policy-makers and the public) that schools are producing desired results through clear goals, progress indicators, measures, analysis of data, reporting procedures, help for participants not meeting goals, and consequences and sanctions. These accountability methods will, it is argued, make the need for continuous improvement clear. The impact of these processes will be system-wide and views from all levels in the system will be required, including at the federal, district, school, classroom and students levels. The ASQ (2008) draws on the work of Andersen and Fagerhaug (2002) to suggest an eight-step process for creating a new performance measurement. The eight steps of the design process are:

1. *Understand and map business structures and processes.* This forces those setting out to design a performance measurement system to think through and reacquaint themselves with the organization, its competitive position, the environment it exists in and its business processes.
2. *Develop business performance priorities.* The performance measurement system should support the stakeholders' requirements from the organization's strategy through to its business processes.
3. *Understand the current performance measurement system.* Every organization has some kind of measurement system in place. For this reason, there are basically two ways to approach the design and implementation of a new performance measurement system.
4. *Develop performance indicators.* The most important element of a performance measurement system is the set of performance indicators you will use to measure your organization's performance and business processes.
5. *Decide how to collect the required data.* Developing perfect performance indicators that will tell you everything you ever wanted to know about what goes on in your organization is one thing, but being able to collect the data required to calculate these performance indicators is a completely different matter.
6. *Design reporting and performance data presentation formats.* In this step, you decide how the performance data will be presented to the users; how the users should apply the performance data for management, monitoring and improvement; and who will have access to performance data.
7. *Test and adjust the performance measurement system.* Your first pass at the performance measurement system will probably not be completely right – there

are bound to be performance indicators that do not work as intended, conflicting indicators, undesirable behaviour and problems with data availability.

8. ***Implement the performance measurement system.*** Now it's time to put your system   to use. This is when the system is officially in place and all can start using it.

(adapted from Andersen and Fagerhaug, 2002)

A further example of the increasing interest in systems reform in the US is provided by the Forum on Educational Accountability, which advances a set of recommendations grounded in six guiding principles for a steadily improving educational system:

> Principle I: Equity and Capacity Building for Student Learning
> Help states, districts, and schools fulfil their educational responsibilities to foster student learning and development by ensuring that all students have equitable access to the resources, tools and information they need to succeed and by building capacity to improve teaching and learning.
> Principle II: Comprehensive State and Local Assessment Systems
> Construct comprehensive and coherent systems of state and local assessments of student learning, that work together to support instruction, educational improvement and accountability.
> Principle III: Assessment and Accountability for Diverse Populations
> Shape the design, construction and application of assessment systems so they are appropriate for an increasingly diverse student population.
> Principle IV: Fair Appraisal of Academic Performance
> Use multiple sources of evidence to describe and interpret school and district performance fairly, based on a balance of progress toward and success in meeting student academic learning targets.
> Principle V: Fair Accountability Decisions
> Improve the validity and reliability of criteria used to classify the performance of schools and districts to ensure fair evaluations and to minimize bias in accountability decisions.
> Principle VI: Use of Assessment and Accountability Information to Improve Schools and Student Learning
> Provide effective, targeted assistance to schools correctly identified as needing assistance.

(Forum on Educational Accountability, 2007)

One example of a current quality and accountability framework operant at state level is the Commonwealth of Pennsylvania (Pennsylvania Department of Education, 2007), which operates a continuous school improvement framework, first introduced in 2003. The design emphasizes a continuous improvement process that can be used by all schools, regardless of current level of performance. The process is split into three phases for developing a results-focused continuous school improvement plan. In the first phase, schools are required to organize and review data including summative, formative and perceptual. In the second phase schools use their analysis of data to discover the 'root cause' of problems. The third and final phase is that of planning solutions, which lays out the detailed action steps to be taken using a clear action sequence (Pennsylvania Department of Education, 2007). The design provides a common framework for work at all levels: school, district, Intermediate Unit (IU) and state levels. This common set of 'organizers' ensures state-wide consistency and coherence in the design of programs, tools, technical assistance and targeted supports.

In a similar fashion, the Commonwealth of Massachusetts Office of Educational Quality and Accountability (EQA) has produced an 'examination' which reviews six essential components of educational management to determine the quality of schools and school systems. Within this framework the determinations of a district's success at improving student performance is based on six accountability standards:

1.   leadership;
2.   curriculum and instruction;
3.   assessment and evaluation systems;
4.   Student Academic Support Systems;
5.   human resource management and professional development;
6.   financial systems and efficient asset management.

(Commonwealth of Massachusetts, 2008)

The frameworks tend to mirror the focus on school improvement planning that was increasingly ubiquitous in the UK commencing in the late 1980s. Nonetheless, US states are working within an increasingly centralized policy system based on the ambitious requirements of the No Child Left Behind Act (US Congress, 2002) which, in many ways, reveals similar commitments to quality as those espoused by the UK and other governments.

New frameworks for inspection and evaluation: balancing external and internal quality and accountability processes

We have examined the issue of internal and external inspection in detail earlier in this text and it seems likely that the balance between these two forms of quality regime is likely to continue to be a focus for debate. To reprise some of these issues we may note that Earley (1998) presented the cases for external and self-assessment and noted that school inspection under Ofsted continued to generate discussion and controversy. In a contribution to the wider debate about the role and function of Ofsted inspection, Earley offered persuasive arguments for increased reliance on school internal quality processes in order to enhance school improvement strategies and raise standards. More specifically he raised critical questions relating to the impact Ofsted was having on schools, particularly in terms of the extent to which external inspection was leading to school improvement. This conception was supported by the work of Learmouth (2000) who traced the development of different forms of school inspection and explored the impact of inspection on schools in difficulties. His analysis of the research and other evidence on the ways in which schools improve raised further questions about the efficacy of external inspection regimes.

Equally, Ferguson *et al.* (2000) examined the relationship between school inspection and school improvement in order to show how headteachers used inspectors' reports to put in place school improvement plans and strategies, and in so doing made a cogent case for developing a culture of self-inspection. Their work suggested there was a powerful impetus for change and that there were alternative approaches to school assessment and improvement, which could work more effectively by encouraging schools to develop their own evaluation processes which, they suggested, should play a greater part in the arrangements for inspection in a movement characterized as 'the self-inspecting school'.

One of the most powerful voices for such a shift in emphasis has been the work of MacBeath, commencing with an influential text that argued that schools should find their own voice through self-assessment (MacBeath, 1999). MacBeath and McGlynn (2002) subsequently argued that self-evaluation in schools sat at the top of the national agenda in response to an awareness that performance tables and inspectors' reports can only tell a partial story. In alignment with changes in the Ofsted regime MacBeath and McGlynn suggested that crucial questions should be asked through internal accountability processes, such as 'How are we doing?' and 'How do we know?' in order to demystify school self-evaluation, so that schools could become self-critical and self-confident. Subsequently MacBeath and MacBeath (2002) offered practical tools to facilitate self-evaluation in a move which aligned with increasing requirements for such internal processes by national inspections agencies. The movement to light touch external inspection, outlined earlier in this text, has given even greater impetus to internal evaluation processes, which have now become a requirement in all schools (MacBeath, 2006).

In response to this research-based critique, the government organization responsible for inspections in England was reframed in 2007 to become 'The Office for Standards in Education, Children's Services and Skills', a new organization which brings together expertise from predecessor inspectorates but retains the name Ofsted. The new Ofsted covers the regulation and inspection of daycare and children's social care, and the inspection of children's services, schools, colleges, initial teacher training, work-based learning, and adult education.

The Strategic Plan for 2007–10 for the new Ofsted sets out how the organization discharges its responsibilities and emphasizes that listening to stakeholders will be fundamental to the way that it operates (Ofsted, 2007). The Education and Inspections Act 2006, which established the new Ofsted, sets out three overriding considerations which Ofsted are to bear in mind, which are to:

- promote improvement in the services we inspect or regulate;
- ensure that these services focus on the interests of the children, parents, adult learners and employers who use them;
- see that these services are efficient and effective.

(HMSO, 2006)

In an attempt to ensure independence, Ofsted does not report to government ministers but directly to Parliament, and to the Lord Chancellor about children and family courts administration. Ofsted has also introduced a new approach to inspection that is intended to be 'light touch'. Moreover, Ofsted has moved towards the integration of the inspections of welfare and education for schools with boarding provision or children's homes that offer education. This integrated approach results in a single inspection report covering both areas, although additional welfare inspections are still possible as necessary where inspection outcomes or other evidence is needed (Ofsted, 2008a: 4). The inspection and report take a holistic approach to the education and welfare provision of children and young people and the new approach is intended to cause less disruption and reduce bureaucracy (Ofsted, 2008a: 5). In addition Ofsted has indicated a series of proposals for future development including to:

- develop proposals to inspect good and outstanding schools once within a six year period;
- trial unannounced inspections;
- take forward proposals for school level surveys of the views of parents and pupils;
- trial the use of staff surveys in pilot inspections;
- test out a greater focus on the achievement of different groups of pupils;
- develop and test criteria, descriptors and guidance for a separate judgement about the school's capacity to improve;
- use contextual value-added (CVA) measures as an important source of information about the progress of pupils;
- explore how inspectors' recommendations might focus more precisely on the actions a school should take to become good or better.

(Ofsted, 2008b: 7)

These proposals reveal a continued commitment to an increased reliance on school self-inspection processes with briefer, less frequent external inspection. This localization of quality measures is balanced by a growing emphasis on metrics that analyse contextual value-added data and the possibility of short but unannounced inspections. This commitment has been reaffirmed in Ofsted annual reports, which state that improvement starts from robust and penetrating self-evaluation, based on good data that are used effectively to identify areas of underperformance, and a shrewd analysis of the implications for individuals and groups. The role of inspection and other forms of external assessment has thus become one of testing out the rigour of self-evaluation and in confirming key areas for action (Ofsted, 2008c: 74). The extent to which this approach decreases or increases the stress that may be felt by schools under inspection has yet to be tested fully but it is clear that the general trend is towards an approach of the kind that might fit within the wider model of continuous improvement described in Chapter 1.

Using students to enhance quality

We have already noted that pupils and students have long been missing as a driver for quality in education. Traditional notions of accountability and quality have emphasized the voice of professionals, such as teachers and lecturers, or external agents, such as advisers and inspectors, in school and college evaluation and improvement (MacBeath, 1999). Ideas pertaining to the importance of student voice have gained significant support in recent years, with a growing number of studies suggesting that active involvement of students in leadership and management decisions assists in school effectiveness and improvement in both the UK (Ruddock and Flutter, 2003; Flutter and Ruddock, 2004) and the US (Mitra, 2008). Strategies for the involvement of students take a variety of forms, including using students to act as researchers to improve learning (Fielding and Bragg, 2003) and a variety of forms of student consultation such as a commitment to the inclusion of students in formal leadership and management structures (Ruddock and Flutter, 2003; Ruddock and McIntyre, 2007). These attitudes align with and show increasing commitment to constructivist forms of leadership for learning that have been evident increasingly in both the UK and North America (Silcock and Brundrett, 2002, 2006). The influence of this work has impacted on schools but is also evident in higher education, especially in connection with teacher education (see, for instance Rand and Shelton, 2002).

Balancing quality, accountability and autonomy

The era of quality and accountability that has characterized educational debate, policy making and practice for the last 20 years has tended to emphasize technical rationalist approaches to school leadership and management. The dominant paradigms of educational discourse have been those of effectiveness and improvement, which find at least some of their roots in a contemporary obsession with quality as measured in examinations, testing and other 'hard' performance indicators. We have argued that this has been to the detriment of older forms of school organization which were based on a more 'dilettante' approach to school leadership (Brundrett, 2000) with an allied acceptance that teachers should be autonomous professionals. It may or may not be fanciful to suggest that the global financial crisis that commenced in 2008 has raised questions about the dominance of business models of leadership and management in the social sciences, including education. One of the most perceptive of recent commentators on school leadership has argued for a fundamental rebalancing of the theory and practice of educational leadership which accepts that leadership is not a science but an applied art (English, 2007). In their impressive analysis of the politics of the professionalism of teachers McCulloch *et al.* (2000) have argued that notions of professionalism are constantly adjusted and recreated in the light of changing circumstance and prevailing policy. It may be that we will witness another radical shift in attitudes to professionalism that will reinvigorate the concept of the autonomous professional in light of a desire to minimize the costs of quality and accountability and a desire to encourage the creative rather than the technical in approaches to education.

Conclusion

In this text we have attempted to address a series of issues relating to the complex and inter-related concepts of quality and accountability. In so doing we have been mindful that these issues have become foregrounded internationally over the period since the

1970s, as governments and their agencies have attempted to focus education systems on the delivery of strategies to enhance effectiveness. Inevitably, education systems have drawn on the wider business literature in order to develop concepts and methods to enhance quality. To some, this process has been anathema since there is a line of argument which states that the adoption of business models in education and other social settings is misplaced. We respect this critique but we are also conscious that many in the academic community involved in the study of educational leadership feel that the careful selection of approaches that have been employed successfully in the business sector is a sensible choice in an era when many schools systems have increasingly encouraged the self-management of schools, with the concomitant effect that schools have themselves become something akin to small- to medium-sized businesses. Moreover, it has become accepted increasingly that schools and colleges should be accountable for the value that they provide in relation to the very large percentage of public funding that they now consume in all developed countries.

The problematic nature of quality and accountability systems was deepened by the original formulation of many quality systems, which developed as centralized systems which emphasized external inspection. For many teachers and lecturers and their representative organizations this appeared to challenge cherished notions of professional autonomy. Happily in recent years there has been a notable movement towards enhanced internal quality mechanisms and a lighter touch in external inspections. Alongside these developments it is notable that there is increasing interest in the role of students in articulating their own attitudes to the education system which, to some extent at least, should belong to them.

It is dangerous to assume that quality and accountability systems in education have reached maturity. Indeed there are signs that systems will continue to adapt and change in order to integrate new demands from central government agencies and society at large. Public attitudes to education have elements which are remarkably stable but expectations do change over time. For instance, as we have outlined in this final chapter, we may note an increasing stress on system-wide leadership and accountability allied to a growing interest in the personalization of learning. Future challenges are, by definition, outside the purview of all but the most foresighted of commentators. However, in an era of financial challenge brought about by a global financial crisis, it seems inevitable that the increasing investment in education that characterized the field internationally during the late 1990s and 2000s is likely to be replaced with a period of relatively declining resource. This being the case, it seems inevitable that one of the main challenges of the future will be to enhance quality whilst ensuring value for money. Moreover, it is possible that we are entering a period when the purpose of education may be re-evaluated in such a way that approaches to quality and accountability may be completely re-evaluated in turn, and it even seems possible that the era of performativity may be coming to an end to be replaced by softer, more creative approaches to school leadership and management.

References

Addison, R. and Brundrett, M. (2008) 'Motivation and demotivation of teachers in primary schools: the challenge of change', *Education 3–13*, 36(1): 79–94.

Adelman, N.E. and Panton Walking-Eagle, K. (1997) 'Teachers, time and school reform', in A. Hargreaves (ed.) *ASCD Yearbook: rethinking educational change with heart and mind*, Virginia: Association for Supervision and Curriculum Development.

Ainley, P. and Bailey, J. (1997) *The Business of Learning: staff and student experiences of further education in the 1990s*, London: Cassell.

Ainscow, M. and West, M. (2006) *Improving Urban Schools: leadership and collaboration*, Maidenhead: Open University Press.

Alexander, F.K. (2000) 'The changing face of accountability: monitoring and assessing institutional performance in higher education', *The Journal of Higher Education*, 71(4): 411–31.

ALI/Ofsted (2005) *The Common Inspection Framework for Education and Training from 2005*, London: ALI/Ofsted.

Allder, M. (1993) 'The meaning of school ethos', *Westminster Studies in Education*, 16: 59–69.

Alvesson, M. (1993) *Cultural Perspectives on Organisations*, Cambridge: Cambridge University Press.

Alvik, T. (1997) *School Self-Evaluation: a whole school approach*, Dundee: CIDREE.

American Society for Quality (2008) *Quality Progress*. Online. Available http://www.asq.org/pub/qualityprogress/past/0202/112oneGoodIdea0202.html (accessed September 2008).

Andersen, B. and Fagerhaug, T. (2002) *Performance Measurement Explained*, Milwaukee, WI: ASQ Quality Press.

Anderson, L. (2005) 'Decentralization, autonomy and school improvement', in M. Coleman and P. Earley (eds) *Leadership and Management in Education: cultures, change and context*, Oxford: Oxford University Press.

Angus, L. (2006) 'Educational leadership and the imperative of including student voices, student interests, and students' lives in the mainstream', *International Journal of Leadership in Education*, 9(4): 369–79.

Avis, J. (2001) 'Educational research, the teacher researcher and social justice', *Education and Social Justice*, 3(3): 34–42.

Ball, C. (1985) *Fitness for Purpose: essays in higher education*, Guildford: SREH and NFER-Nelson.

Ball, S.J. (1990) 'Management as a moral technology', in S.J. Ball (ed.) *Foucault and Education*, London: Routledge.

—— (2001) *Sociology of Education*, London: RoutledgeFalmer.

Barber, M. (1997) *The Learning Game: arguments for an education revolution*, London: Indigo.

Barth, R. (1986) 'On sheep and goats and school reform', *Phi Delta Kappan*, 68(4): 293–96.

—— (1990) *Improving Schools from Within*, San Francisco: Jossey-Bass.

—— (2001) 'Teacher leader', *Phi Delta Kappan*, 82(6): 443–49.

Bartlett, S. (2002) 'An evaluation of the work of a group of best practice teacher researchers', *Journal of In-Service Education*, 28(3): 527–40.

Bastiani, J. (2002) *Parental Involvement in Children's Learning: a practical framework for review and development of home-school work*, London: Tower Hamlets Education.

Beatty, B. (2000) 'Teachers leading their own professional growth: self-directed reflection and collaboration and changes in perception of self and work in secondary school teachers', *Journal of In-Service Education*, 26: 73–97.

Becher, T., Eraut, M., Barton, J., Canning, T. and Knight, J. (1979) *Accountability in the Middle Years of Schooling: an analysis of policy options*, East Sussex LEA/University of Sussex Research Project, Brighton: University of Sussex.

Belfield, C. and Thomas, H. (2000) 'The relationship between resources and performance in further education colleges', *Oxford Review of Education*, 26(2): 239–53.

Bell, L., Bolam, R. and Cubillo, L. (2003) 'A systematic review of the impact of school leadership and management on student outcomes', in *Research Evidence in Education Library*, London: EPPI-Centre Social Science Research Unit, Institute of Education.

Bennett, R. (2003) 'Determinants of undergraduate student drop out rates in a university business studies department', *Journal of Further and Higher Education*, 27(2): 123–41.

Benson, S. (2002) *Leading Learning: instructional leadership in infants schools*, Full Practitioner Report, Nottingham: National College for School Leadership.

Berger, L.A. and Berger, D.R. (2004) *The Talent Management Handbook*, New York: McGraw-Hill.

Bezzina, C. (2008) 'Towards a learning community: the journey of a Maltese Catholic Church School', *Management in Education*, 22(3): 22–27.

Biggs, J.B. (1992) 'Returning to school: review and discussion', in A. Demetriou, M. Shayer and A. Efklides (eds) *Neo-Piagetian Theories of Cognitive Development: implications and applications for education*, London: Routledge.

Bird, S. (2003) *Do the Right Thing! How governors can contribute to community cohesion and accountability*, TEN – The Education Network and the Department for Education and Skills, Nottingham: Department for Education and Skills Publications.

Blase, J. and Blase, J. (2004) *Handbook of Instructional Leadership: how successful principals promote teaching and learning*, Thousand Oaks, CA: Corwin Press.

Bodine, E., Fuller, B., Gonzalez, M., Huerta, L., Naughton, S., Park, S. and Teh, L.W. (2008) 'Disparities in charter school resources – the influence of state policy and community', *Journal of Education Policy*, 23(1): 1–33.

Bolam, R. (2000) 'Emerging policy trends: some implications for continuing professional development', *Journal of In-Service Education*, 26(2): 267–80.

Bolam, R., McMahon, A., Stoll, L., Thomas, S. and Wallace, M. (2005) *Creating and Sustaining Effective Professional Learning Communities*, Research Report 637, London: Department for Education and Skills.

Bossert, S., Dwyer, D., Rowan, B. and Lee, G. (1982). 'The instructional management role of the principal', *Educational Administration Quarterly*, 18(3): 34–64.

Boyle, B., Lamprianou, I. and Boyle, T. (2005) 'A longitudinal study of teacher change: What makes professional development effective? Report of the second year of the study', *School Effectiveness and School Improvement*, 16(1): 1–27.

Bredeson, P.V. and Johansson, O. (2000) 'The school principal's role in teacher professional development', *Journal of In-Service Education*, 26(2): 385–401.

Briggs, A.R.J. (2005) 'Making a difference: an exploration of leadership roles within sixth form colleges in maintaining ethos within a context of change', *British Educational Research Journal*, 31(2): 223–38.

Broadfoot, P. (2000) 'Liberating the learner through assessment', in J. Collins and D. Cook (eds) *Understanding Learning: influences and outcomes*, London: Paul Chapman Publishing.

Brooks, R. (2004) '"My mum would be as pleased as punch if I actually went, but my dad seems a bit more particular about it": parental involvement in young people's higher education choices', *British Educational Research Journal*, 30(4): 495–514.

Brundrett, M. (2000) *Beyond Competence: the challenge for educational management*, King's Lynn: Peter Francis Publishing.

Brundrett, M. and Crawford, M. (2008) (eds) *Developing School Leaders: an international perspective*, London: Routledge.

Brundrett, M. and Silcock, P. (2002) *Achieving Competence, Success and Excellence in Teaching*, London: Routledge.

Brundrett, M. and Terrell, I. (2004) (eds) *Learning to Lead in the Secondary School: becoming an effective head of department*, London: RoutledgeFalmer.

Bullock, A. and Thomas, H. (1997) *Schools at the Centre?* London: Routledge.

Burchell, H., Dyson, J. and Rees, M. (2002) 'Making a difference: a study of the impact of continuing professional development on professional practice', *Journal of In-Service Education*, 28(2): 219–29.

Burton, N. and Brundrett, M. (2005) *Leading the Curriculum in the Primary School*, London: Sage.

Bush, T. (2003) *Theories of Educational Management and Leadership*, London: Paul Chapman Publishing.

—— (2008) *Leadership and Management Development in Education*, London: Sage.

Bush, T. and Glover, D. (2004) *Leadership Development: evidence and beliefs,* Summary Report, Nottingham: NCSL.

Busher, H. (1998) 'Educational leadership and management: contexts, theory and practice', in P. Clough (ed.) (1998) *Managing Special and Inclusive Education*, London: Paul Chapman Publishing.

—— (2006) *Understanding Educational Leadership: people, power and culture*, Maidenhead: Open University Press.

Busher, H. and Saran, R. (2000) 'Managing with support staff', in K. Stott and V. Trafford (eds) *Partnerships: shaping the future of education*, London: Middlesex University Press.

Butt, G. and Lance, A. (2005) 'Modernizing the roles of support staff in primary schools: changing focus, changing function', *Educational Review*, 57(2): 139–49.

Byham, W., Smith, A. and Paese, M. (2003) *Grow Your Own Leaders*, London: Financial Times/Prentice Hall.

Campbell, J. and Li, M. (2008) 'Asian students' voices: an empirical study of Asian students' learning experiences at a New Zealand University', *Journal of Studies in International Education*, 12(4): 375–96.

Capper, C. and Jamison, M. (1993) 'Let the buyer beware: total quality management and educational research and practice', *Educational Researcher*, 22(3): 15–30.

Carmichael, R., Palermo, J., Reeve, L. and Vallence, K. (2001) 'Student learning: "the heart of quality" in education and training', *Assessment and Evaluation in Higher Education*, 26(5): 449–63.

Carr, W. and Kemmis, S. (1986) *Becoming Critical: education, knowledge and action research*, London: Falmer Press.

Catelli, L., Padovano, K. and Costello, J. (2000) 'Action research in the context of a school-university partnership: its value, problems, issues and benefits', *Educational Action Research*, 8(2): 225–42.

Chapman, C. (2001) 'Unlocking the potential: inspection as a mechanism for school improvement', *Improving Schools*, 4(3): 41–50.

—— (2002) *Ofsted and School Improvement: teachers' perceptions of the inspection process in schools facing challenging circumstances*, Coventry: University of Warwick Institute of Education.

—— (2004) 'Leadership for improvement in urban and challenging contexts', *London Review of Education*, 2(2): 95–108.

CHES (Centre for Higher Education Studies) (1994) *Assessment of the Quality of Higher Education: a review and an evaluation*, London: University of London, Institute of Education.

Children's Services and Skills Strategic Plan 2007–10, London: Ofsted.

Clegg, S. and McNulty, K. (2002) 'Partnership working in delivering social inclusion: organisational and gender dynamics', *Journal of Education Policy*, 17(5): 587–601.

Cochran-Smith, M. and Lytle, S. (1999) 'Teacher learning communities', *Review of Research in Education*, 24(4): 24–32.

Coleman, M. (2005) 'Evaluation in education', in M. Coleman and P. Earley, *Leadership and Management in Education: cultures, change and context*, Oxford: Oxford University Press.

Coleman, M. and Earley, P. (2005) *Leadership and Management in Education: cultures, change and context*, Oxford: Oxford University Press.

Collinson, D. (2007) (ed.) *Leadership and the Learner Voice*, Lancaster: Lancaster University Management School, Centre for Excellence in Leadership.

Commonwealth of Massachusetts Office of Educational Quality and Accountability (2008) *The EQA Examination Process*. Online. Available http://eqa.mass.edu/home/index.asp (accessed January 2009).

Connor, H. (2001) 'Deciding for or against participation in higher education: the views of young people from lower social class backgrounds', *Higher Education Quarterly*, 55(2): 204–24.

Court, M. (2004) 'Talking back to new public management versions of accountability in education', *Educational Management Administration and Leadership*, 32(2): 171–94.

Cox, B. and Ingleby, A. (1997) *Practical Pointers for Quality Assessment*, London: Kogan Page.

Coyle, P. (2003) 'The balance of autonomy and accountability in London Guildhall University's quality-management system', *Quality in Higher Education*, 9(2): 199–205.

Cranston, N.C. (2007) 'Through the eyes of potential aspirants: another view of the principalship', *School Leadership and Management*, 27(2): 109–28.

Cray, D. and Mallory, G. (1998) *Making Sense of Managing Culture*, London: International Thompson Business Press.

Creemers, B. (1994) *The Effective Classroom*, London: Cassell.

Crosby, P.B. (1979) *Quality is Free: the art of making quality certain*, New York: McGraw-Hill.

Crozier, G. and Davies, J. (2007) 'Hard to reach parents or hard to reach schools? A discussion of home-school relationships with particular reference to Bangladeshi and Pakistani parents', *British Educational Research Journal*, 33(3): 295–313.

Cruddas, L. (2007) 'Engaged voices – dialogic interaction and the construction of shared social meanings', *Educational Action Research*, 15(3): 479–88.

Cuban, L. (1988) *The Managerial Imperative and the Practice of Leadership in Schools*, Albany, NY: SUNY Press.

Dale, B.G. and Plunkett, J.J. (1991) *Quality Costing*, London: Chapman and Hall.

Davies, B. and Ellison, L. (1997) (eds) *School Leadership for the 21st Century: a competency and knowledge approach,* London: Routledge.

Davies, D. and Rudd, P. (2001) *Evaluating School Self-Evaluation*, Slough: NFER.

Davies, P. and Scribbins, K. (1985) *Marketing Further and Higher Education*, Harlow: Longman.

Davies, R. and Preston, M. (2002) 'An evaluation of the impact of continuing professional development on personal and professional lives', *Journal of In-Service Education*, 28(2): 231–54.

Davis, A. and White, J. (2001) 'Accountability and school inspection: in defence of audited self-review', *Journal of Philosophy of Education*, 35(4): 667–81.

Day, C. (1999) *Developing Teachers: the challenge of lifelong learning*, London: Falmer Press.

—— (2003) 'Successful leadership in the twenty-first century', in A. Harris, C. Day, D. Hopkins, M. Hadfield, A. Hargreaves and C. Chapman (eds) *Effective Leadership for School Improvement*, London: RoutledgeFalmer.

—— (2004) 'The passion of successful leadership', *School Leadership and Management*, 24(4): 425–37.

Day, C., Hadfield, M. and Kellow, M. (2002) 'Schools as learning communities: building capacity through network learning', *Education 3–13*, 30(3): 19–22.

Day, C., Harris, A. and Hadfield, M. (2001) 'Grounding knowledge of schools in stakeholder realities: a multi-perspective study of effective school leaders', *School Leadership and Management*, 21(1): 19–42.

Day, C., Sammons, P., Hopkins, D., Harris, A., Leithwood, K., Qing, G., Penlington, C., Mehta, P. and Kington, A. (2007) *The Impact of School Leadership on Pupil Outcomes: interim report*, Research Report DCSF-RR018, Nottingham: University of Nottingham.

De Grauwe, A. (2005) 'Improving the quality of education through school-based management: learning from international experiences', *International Review of Education*, 51(4): 269–87.

Deal, T. and Kennedy, A. (1988) *Corporate Cultures*, London: Penguin.

Dean, P. (2001) 'Blood on the tracks: an accusation and proposal', *Journal of In-Service Education*, 27(3): 491–500.

Deem, R. (1998) 'New managerialism and higher education: the management of performances and cultures in UK universities', *International Studies in the Sociology of Education*, 8(1), 47–70.

Deem, R. and Brehony, K.J. (2005) 'Management as ideology: the case of "new managerialism" in higher education', *Oxford Review of Education*, 31(2), 217–35.

Demie, F. (2003) 'Using value-added data for school self-evaluation: a case study of practice in inner city schools', *School Leadership and Management*, 23(4), 445–67.

Deming, W.E. (1982) *Out of Crisis*, Cambridge, MA: MIT.

DES (Department of Education and Science Ireland) (2003a) *Looking at Our School: an aid to self-evaluation in primary schools*, Dublin: DES.

—— (2003b) *Looking at Our School: an aid to self-evaluation in second level schools*, Dublin: DES.

Devos, G. and Verhoeven, J. (2003) 'School self-evaluation: conditions and caveats', *Educational Management and Administration*, 31(4), 403–20.

DfEE (Department for Education and Employment) (1997) *Excellence in Schools*, London: HMSO.

—— (1998a) *Teachers: meeting the challenge of change*, London: Stationery Office.

—— (1998b) *Governors Guide to Law*, London: HMSO.

—— (1998c) *The Learning Age: a renaissance for a new Britain*, London: Stationery Office.

—— (1998d) *Further Education in the New Millennium*, London: Stationery Office.

—— (2000a) *Performance Management in Schools: performance management framework*, London: Stationery Office.

—— (2000b) *Performance Management in Schools: model performance management policy*, London: Stationery Office.

—— (2000c) *Statistics of Education: teachers in England and Wales 2000*, London: Stationery Office.

DfEE and Ofsted (1995) *Governing Bodies and Effective Schools*, London: Ofsted.

DfES (Department for Education and Skills) (2001a) *Learning and Teaching: a strategy for professional development*, London: Stationery Office.

—— (2001b) *Schools Achieving Success*, London: Stationery Office.

—— (2002) *14–19: Extending Opportunities and Raising Standards: summary document*, London: Stationery Office.

—— (2003a) *Time for Standards: guidance accompanying the regulations issued under the Education Act 2002*, Nottingham: DfES.

—— (2003b) *Every Child Matters: change for children in schools*, London: DfES.

—— (2003c) *Excellence and Enjoyment: a strategy for primary schools*, London: DfES.

—— (2003d) *Statutory Guidance on School Governance*, London: DfES.

—— (2003e) *Every Child Matters*, (CM5860), Norwich: HMSO.

—— (2004a) Department for Education and Skills, *National Standards for Headteachers*, London: Stationery Office.

—— (2004b) 'Personalised learning: building a new relationship with schools', Miliband Press Notice 2004/0002. Online. Available http://www.dfes.gov.uk/pns (accessed January 2009).

—— (2004c) *A New Relationship with Schools: improving performance through school self-evaluation*, Nottingham: DfES Publications.

—— (2005a) *Education Improvement Partnerships: local collaboration for school improvement and better service delivery*, Nottingham: Department for Education and Skills.

—— (2005b) *Higher Standards, Better Schools for All: more choice for parents and pupils*, London: Stationery Office.

—— (2006) *Best Practice in Self-Evaluation: a survey of schools, colleges and Local Authorities*, Report Reference HMI 2533. Online. Available http://www.ofsted.gov.uk/publications (accessed October 2009).

Dimmock, C. (2000) *Designing the Learning-Centred School: a cross-cultural perspective*, London: Falmer Press.

Dimmock, C. and Walker, A. (2004) 'A new approach to strategic leadership: learning-centredness, connectivity and cultural context in school design', *School Leadership and Management*, 24(1): 39–56.

Dobson, P. and Starkey, K. (1993) *The Strategic Management Blueprint*, Oxford: Blackwell Publishers.

Donnelly, C. (2000) 'In pursuit of school ethos', *British Journal of Educational Studies*, 48(2): 134–54.

Down, B., Hogan, C. and Chadbourne, R. (1999) 'Making sense of performance management: official rhetoric and teachers' reality', *Asia-Pacific Journal of Teacher Education*, 27(1): 11–24.

Downes, P. (1997) 'Managing school finance', in B. Davies and L. Ellison (eds) *School Leadership for the 21st Century: a competency and knowledge approach*, London: Routledge.

Draper, J. and McMichael, P. (2003) 'The rocky road to headship', *Australian Journal of Education*, 47(2): 185–96.

DuFour, R. (2004) *Highlights: personalised learning*, DfES. Online. Available www.dfes.gov.uk/highlights/article13.shtml (accessed October 2009).

Duncan, D. (2003) 'Subject leader accountability', in M. Brundrett and I. Terrell (eds) *Learning to Lead in the Secondary School: becoming an effective head of department*, London: RoutledgeFalmer.

Dymoke, S. and Harrison, J.K. (2006) 'Professional development and the beginning teacher: issues of teacher autonomy and institutional conformity in the performance review process', *Journal of Education for Teaching*, 32(1): 71–92.

Earley, P. (1994) *Lecturers' Workload and Factors Affecting Stress Levels*, Slough: National Foundation for Educational Research.

—— (1998) *School Improvement after Inspection: school and LEA responses*, London: British Educational Leadership and Management Society/Paul Chapman Publishing.

Earley, P. and Bubb, S. (2004) *Leading and Managing Continuing Professional Development: developing people, developing schools*, London: Paul Chapman Publishing.

Earley, P., Evans, J., Collarbone, P., Gold, A. and Halpin, D. (2002) *Establishing the Current State of School Leadership in England*, London: Institute of Education, University of London.

Online. Available http://www.dfes.gov.uk/research/data/uploadfiles/RR336.pdf (accessed September 2009).

Ebbutt, D. (2002) 'The development of a research culture in secondary schools', *Educational Action Research*, 10(1): 123–42.

Edwards, A. and Waring, J. (1999) 'Parental involvement in raising the achievement of primary school pupils: why bother?' *Oxford Review of Education*, 25(3): 325–41.

Ellis, R. (1993) *Quality Assurance for University Teaching*, Buckingham: SRHE and Open University Press.

Elmore, R. (2000) *Building a New Structure for School Leadership*, Washington, D.C.: Albert Shanker Institute.

English, F.W. (2007) *The Art of Educational Leadership: balancing performance and accountability*, London: Sage.

ENQA (European Network for Quality Assurance in Higher Education) (2005) *Standards and Guidelines for Quality Assurance in the European Higher Education Area*, Helsinki: ENQA.

Erickson, D. (1967) 'The school administrator', *Review of Educational Research*, 37(4): 417–32.

Evans, L. (2001) 'Delving deeper into morale, job satisfaction and motivation among education professionals: re-examining the leadership dimension', *Educational Management and Administration*, 29(3): 291–306.

Every Child Matters (2003) Department for Education and Skills (CM5860), Norwich: HMSO.

Farnham, D. (1999) *Managing University Staff in Changing University Systems*, Buckingham: Society for Research in Higher Education and Open University Press.

Farrell, C.M. and Law, J. (1999) 'Changing forms of accountability in education? A case study of LEAs in Wales', *Public Administration*, 77(2), 293–310.

FEFC (Further Education Funding Council) (1997) *Teaching and Learning in Further Education: diversity and change*, London: Routldege.

FENTO (Further Education National Training Organisation) (2001) *Standards for Teaching and Supported Learning in Further Education in England and Wales*, London: FENTO.

Ferguson, N., Earley, P., Fidler, B. and Ouston, J. (2000) *Improving Schools and Inspection: the self-inspecting school*, London: Paul Chapman Publishing.

Fielding, M. (1997) 'Beyond school effectiveness and school improvement: lighting the slow fuse of possibility', *The Curriculum Journal*, 8(1): 7–27.

—— (2001) 'Beyond the rhetoric of student voice: new departures or new constraints in the transformation of 21st century schooling?' *Forum for Providing 13–19 Comprehensive Education*, 43(2): 100–110.

—— (2006) 'Leadership, radical student engagement and the necessity of person-centred education', *International Journal of Leadership in Education*, 9(4): 299–313.

Fielding, M. and Bragg, S. (2003) *Consulting Pupils: students as researchers*, London: Pearson.

Fielding, M., Fuller, A. and Loose, T. (1999) 'Taking pupil perspectives seriously: the central place of pupil voice in primary school improvement', in G. Southworth and P. Lincoln (eds) *Supporting Improving Primary Schools: the role of heads and LEAs*, London: Falmer Press.

Fink, D. (2005) *Leadership for Mortals: developing and sustaining leaders of learning*, London: Paul Chapman Publishing.

—— (2010) 'Developing and sustaining leaders of learning', in B. Davies and M. Brundrett (eds) *Developing Successful Leadership*, New York: Springer.

Fink, D. and Brayman, C. (2006) 'School leadership succession and the challenges of change', *Educational Administration Quarterly*, 42(1): 62–89.

Fitzgerald, T. and Gunter, H. (2006) 'Leading learning: middle leadership in schools in England and New Zealand', *Management in Education*, 20(3): 6–8.

Fleming, P. and Amesbury, M. (2001) *The Art of Middle Management in Primary Schools*, London: David Fulton Publishers Ltd.

Flinders, D. (2005) 'The costs of accountability', *Journal of Curriculum Studies*, 37(5): 621–29.

Flutter, J. and Ruddock, J. (2004) *Consulting Pupils: what's in it for schools?* London: Routledge.

Forum on Educational Accountability (2007) *Assessment and Accountability for Improving Schools and Learning: principles and recommendations for federal law and state and local systems made by the expert panel on assessment.* Online. Available www.edaccountability.org (accessed September 2008).

Foskett, R. (2005) 'Collaborative partnership between HE and employers: a study of workforce development', *Journal of Further and Higher Education*, 29(3): 251–64.

Frearson, M. (2002) *Tomorrow's Learning Leaders: developing leadership and management for post-compulsory learning*, 2002 Survey Report, London: Learning and Skills Development Agency.

Friedman, A. and Phillips, M. (2001) 'Leaping the CPD hurdle: a study of the barriers and drivers to participation in continuing professional development', paper presented at the British Educational Research Association Annual Conference, University of Leeds, 13–15 September 2001. Online. Available http://www.leeds.ac.uk/educol/documents/00001892.htm (accessed January 2009).

Frost, D., Frost, R., MacBeath, J. and Pedder, D. (2009) 'The influence and participation of children and young people in their learning (IPiL) project', International Congress for School Effectiveness and Improvement, Vancouver, BC Canada, 4–7 January 2009, 1–14.

Frost, R. (2008) 'Developing student participation, research and leadership: the HCD student partnership', *School Leadership and Management*, 28(4): 353–68.

Frost, R. and Holden, G. (2008) 'Student voice and future schools: building partnerships for student participation', *Improving Schools*, 11(1): 83–95.

Fullan, M. (2001) *Leading in a Culture of Change*, San Francisco, CA: Jossey-Bass.

Further Education Unit (1997) 'Continuous improvement and quality standards', in M. Preedy, R. Glatter and R. Levačić (eds) *Educational Management: strategy, quality and resources*, Buckingham: Open University Press.

Garn, G. (2001) 'Moving from bureaucratic to market accountability: the problem of imperfect information', *Educational Administration Quarterly*, 37(4): 571–99.

Garner, P. (2002) 'Now even more than just a helper: how learning support assistants see their role in schools', *Journal of the College of Teachers*, 52(3): 13–20.

Gaspar, M., Pinto, A., da Conceição, H. and da Silva, J. (2008) 'A questionnaire for listening to students' voices in the assessment of teaching quality in a classical medical school', *Assessment and Evaluation in Higher Education*, 33(4), 445–53.

Gewertz, C. (2003) 'N.Y.C. Chancellor Aims to Bolster Instructional Leadership', *Education Week*, 22(16): 7–12.

Gewirtz, S., Ball, S.J. and Bowe, R. (1995) *Markets, Choice and Education in Education*, Buckingham: Open University Press.

Giddens, A. (1984) *The Constitution of Society*, Cambridge: Polity Press.

Giles, C. (1997) *School Development Planning: a practical guide to the strategic management process*, London: Northcote House.

Gillies, V. (2005) 'Meeting parents' needs? Discourses of "support" and "inclusion" in family policy', *Critical Social Policy*, 25(1): 70–90.

—— (2006) 'Working class mothers and school life: exploring the role of emotional capital', *Gender and Education*, 18(3): 281–93.

Glatter, R. (1997) 'Context and capability in educational management', *Educational Management and Administration*, 25(2): 191–202.

Gleeson, D. and Husbands, C. (2001) (eds) *The Performing School: managing, teaching and learning in a performance culture*, London: RoutledgeFalmer.

Gleeson, D. and Husbands, C. (2003) 'Modernizing schooling through performance management: a critical appraisal', *Journal of Education Policy*, 18(5): 499–511.

Glover, D. and Coleman, M. (2005) 'School culture, climate and ethos: interchangeable or distinctive concepts?' *Journal of In-Service Education*, 31(2): 251–71.

Glover, D. and Law, S. (2004) 'Creating the right learning environment: the application of models of culture to student perceptions of teaching and learning in eleven secondary schools', *School Effectiveness and School Improvement*, 15(3&4): 313–36.

Goldring, E.B. (1997) 'Educational leadership: schools, environments and boundary spanning', in M. Preedy, R. Glatter, and R. Levačić (eds) *Educational Management: strategy, quality and resources*, Buckingham: Open University Press.

Goodlad, S. (1995) *The Quest for Quality: sixteen forms of heresy in higher education*, Buckingham: SRHE and Open University Press.

Gordon, G. (2002) 'The roles of leadership and ownership in building an effective quality culture', *Quality in Higher Education*, 8(1): 97–106.

Gore, J. and Gitlin, A. (2004) '(Re)Visioning the academic-teacher divide: power and knowledge in the educational community', *Teachers and Teaching*, 10(1): 35–58.

Gosling, D. (2000) 'Continuous professional development', *Educational Developments*, 1(2): 11.

Gravatt, J. and Silver, R. (2000) 'Partnerships with the community', in A. Smithers and P. Robinson (eds) *Further Education Re-Formed*, London: Falmer Press.

Gray, J. and Wilcox, B. (1995) *Good School, Bad School*, Buckingham: Open University Press.

Green, D. (1994) (ed.) *What is Quality in Higher Education*, Buckingham: SRHE and Open University Press.

Gronn, P. (2000) 'Distributed properties: a new architecture for leadership', *Educational Management and Administration*, 28(3): 317–38.

—— (2003a) *The New Work of Educational Leaders*, London: Paul Chapman Publishing.

—— (2003b) 'Leadership: who needs it?' *School Leadership and Management*, 23(3): 267–91.

Gross, N. and Herriot, R. (1965) *Staff Leadership in Schools*, New York: Wiley.

GTCE (General Teaching Council for England) (2002) *Teachers on Teaching: a survey of the teaching profession*. Online. Available http://www.educationguardian.co.uk (accessed October 2008).

Gvaramadze, I. (2008) 'From quality assurance to quality enhancement in the European Higher Education Area', *European Journal of Education*, 43(4): 443–55.

Hall, G. and George, A. (1999) 'The impact of principal change facilitator style', in H.J. Freiberg (ed.) *School Climate: measuring, improving and sustaining healthy learning environments*, London: Falmer Press.

Hallinger, P. (2010) 'Developing instructional leadership', in B. Davies and M. Brundrett (eds) *Developing Successful Leadership*, New York: Springer.

Hallinger, P. and Heck, R. (1996) 'Reassessing the principal's role in school effectiveness: a review of the empirical research', *Educational Administration Quarterly*, 32(1): 27–31.

—— (1999) 'Can leadership enhance school effectiveness?', in T. Bush, L. Bell, R. Bolam, R. Glatter and P. Ribbins (eds) *Educational Management: redefining theory, policy and practice*, London: Paul Chapman Publishing.

Hallinger, P. and Snidvongs, K. (2005) *Adding Value to School Leadership and Management: a review of trends in the development of managers in the education and business sectors*. Online. Available http://www.ncsl.org.uk/publications (accessed 10 December 2005).

Halstead, M. (1994) 'Accountability and values', in D. Scott (ed.) *Accountability and Control in Educational Settings*, London: Cassell.

Hammett, N. and Burton, N. (2005) 'Motivation, stress and learning support assistants: an examination of staff perceptions at a rural secondary school', *School Leadership and Management*, 25(3): 299–310.

Handy, C. (1993) *Understanding Organisations*, Harmondsworth: Penguin.

Hannon, P. (2000) 'Rhetoric and research in family literacy', *British Educational Research Journal*, 26(1): 121–38.

Hargreaves, A. and Fink, D. (2006) *Sustainable Leadership*, San Francisco, CA: John Wiley.

Hargreaves, D. (1995) 'School culture, school effectiveness and school improvement', *School Effectiveness and Improvement*, 6(1): 23–46.

—— (2001) 'A capital theory of school effectiveness and school improvement', *British Educational Research Journal*, 27(4): 487–503.

Hargreaves, D. and Hopkins, D. (1994) *Development Planning for School Improvement*, London: Cassell.

Hargreaves, J. and Christou, A. (2002) 'An institutional perspective on QAA subject benchmarking', *Quality Assurance in Education*, 10(3): 187–91.

Harris, A. (2003) 'Teacher leadership as distributed leadership: heresy, fantasy or possibility?' *School Leadership and Management*, 23(3): 313–24.

—— (2004) 'Distributed leadership and school improvement: leading or misleading?' *Educational Management Administration and Leadership*, 32(1): 11–24.

Harris, A. and Chapman, C. (2001) *Leading Schools Facing Challenging Circumstances*, London: Department for Education and Skills.

Harris, A. and Lambert, L. (2003a) *Building Capacity for School Improvement*, Maidenhead: Open University Press.

—— (2003b) *What is Leadership Capacity?* Nottingham: National College for School Leadership.

Harris, A., Muijs, D. and Crawford, M. (2003) 'Deputy and assistant heads: building leadership potential'. Online. Available www.nscl.org.uk/literaturereviews (accessed September 2009).

Hart, R.A. (1997) *Children's Participation: the theory and practice of involving young citizens in community development and environmental care*, London: Earthscan Publications.

Hartle, F. and Thomas, K. (2004) *Growing Tomorrow's School Leaders*. Online. Available http://www.ncsl.org.uk/researchpublications (accessed September 2009).

Hartley, D. (2008) 'Education, markets and the pedagogy of personalisation', *British Journal of Educational Studies*, 56(4): 365–81.

Heck, R. and Marcoulides, G. (1996) 'School culture and performance: testing the invariance of an organisational model', *School Effectiveness and School Improvement*, 7(1): 76–95.

Hemsley-Brown, J. and Oplatka, I. (2006) 'Universities in a competitive global marketplace: a systematic review of the literature on higher education marketing', *International Journal of Public Sector Management*, 19(4): 316–38.

Hendel, D.D. and Lewis, D.R. (2005) 'Quality assurance of higher education in transition countries: accreditation, accountability and assessment', *Tertiary Education and Management*, 11(3): 239–58.

Herman, J. and Winters, L. (1992) *Tracking your School's Success: a guide to sensible evaluation*, Thousand Oaks, CA: Corwin Press.

Hinett, K. and Weeden, P. (2000) 'How am I doing? Developing critical self-evaluation in trainee teachers', *Quality in Higher Education*, 6(3): 245–57.

Hirsch, W. (2000) *Succession Planning Demystified*, Report 372, Brighton: The Institute for Employment Studies.

HMSO (2006) *The Education and Inspections Act*, London: HMSO.

Hodkinson, P. and Bloomer, M. (2000a) 'Stokingham Sixth Form College: institutional culture and dispositions to learning', *British Journal of Sociology of Education*, 21(2): 187–202.

—— (2000b) 'Accountability, audit and exclusion in further and higher education', paper presented at SCUTREA 30th Annual Conference, University of Nottingham 3–5 July 2000.

Online. Available http://www.leeds.ac.uk/educol/documents/00001450.htm (accessed September 2009).

Hodson, P. and Thomas, H. (2003) 'Quality assurance in higher education: fit for the new millennium or simply year 2000 compliant?' *Higher Education*, 45(3): 375–87.

Hoecht, A. (2006) 'Quality assurance in UK higher education: issues of trust, control, professional autonomy and accountability', *Higher Education*, 51(4): 541–63.

Hofman, R., Dukstra, N. and Hofman, A. (2005) 'School self-evaluation instruments: an assessment framework', *International Journal of Leadership in Education*, 8(3): 253–72.

Hollingsworth, A. (2004) *The School as a Learning Community*, International Research Associate Perspective Report, Nottingham: National College for School Leadership.

Hopfl, H. (2000) 'Getting to the heart of HRD: some matters of quality and performance in higher education in the UK', *Human Resource Development International*, 3(2), 195–206.

Howson, J. (2007) *The State of the Labour Market for Senior Staff in Schools in England and Wales 2006–2007*. Online. Available http://www.educationdatasurveys.org.uk (accessed 21 April 2007).

Hoyle, E. and Wallace, M. (2005) *Educational Leadership: ambiguity, professionals and managerialism*, London: Sage Publications.

Huisman, J. and Currie, J. (2004) 'Accountability in higher education: bridge over troubled water?' *Higher Education*, 48(4): 529–51.

Humphreys, K. and Susak, Z. (1999) 'Learning how to fish: issues for teachers engaging in self-evaluation and reflective enquiry in school', *Research in Education*, 64(2): 78–90.

Hyland, T. and Matlay, H. (1998) 'Lifelong learning and new deal vocationalism', *British Journal of Educational Studies*, 46(4): 399–414.

Hyland, T. and Merrill, B. (2001) 'Community, partnership and social inclusion in further education', *Journal of Further and Higher Education*, 25(3): 337–48.

Institute of Education (2003) *Improving Teaching and Learning in Higher Education*, London: Institute of Education.

Jackson, D. and Payne, G. (2002) *The Headteacher – guardian of leverage for school improvement*, Nottingham: National College for School Leadership.

James, C., Connolly, M., Dunning, G. and Elliott, T. (2006) *How Very Effective Primary Schools Work*, London: Paul Chapman Publishing.

Johnson, B. (2003) 'Teacher collaboration: good for some, not so good for others', *Educational Studies*, 29(4): 337–50.

Johnson, R.N. and Deem, R. (2003) 'Talking of students: tensions and contradictions for the manager-academic and the university in contemporary higher education', *Higher Education*, 46(3): 289–314.

Johnstone, B. (2004) 'The economics and politics of cost sharing in higher education: comparative perspectives', *Economics of Education Review*, 23(4): 403–10.

Joyce, B., Calhoun, E. and Hopkins, D. (1999) *The New Structure of School Improvement: inquiring schools and achieving students*, Buckingham: Open University Press.

Juran, J.M. (1989) *Juran on Leadership for Quality: an executive handbook*, New York: The Free Press.

Karagiorgi, Y. and Symeou, L. (2006) 'Teacher professional development in Cyprus: reflections on current trends and challenges in policy and practices', *Journal of In-Service Education*, 32(1): 47–61.

Keating, I. and Moorcroft, R. (2006) *Managing the Business of Schools*, London: Paul Chapman Publishing.

Keedy, J.L. (1999) 'Examining teacher instructional leadership within the small group dynamics of collegial groups', *Teaching and Teacher Education*, 15(7): 785–99.

Kells, H.R. (1995) 'Creating a culture of evaluation and self-regulation in higher education organizations', *Total Quality Management*, 6(5/6): 457–67.

Kelly, S., White, M.I. and Rouncefield, M. (2005) *Explicating Leadership*, Centre for Excellence in Leadership: University of Lancaster.

Kennedy, A. (2005) 'Models of continuing professional development: a framework for analysis', *Journal of In-Service Education*, 31(2): 235–50.

Kennedy, H. (1997) *Learning Works: widening participation in further education*, Coventry: Further Education Funding Council.

Kennewell, S., Parkinson, J. and Tanner, H. (2000) *Developing the ICT Capable School*, London: RoutledgeFalmer.

Khan, F. (2006) 'Who participates in school councils and how?' *Prospects*, 36(1): 97–119.

Kinder, K., Harland, J. and Wootten, M. (1991) *The Impact of School Focused INSET on Classroom Practice*, Slough: National Foundation for Educational Research.

Kirkwood, A. and Price, L. (2005) 'Learners and learning in the twenty-first century: what do we know about students' attitudes towards and experiences of information and communication technologies that will help us design courses?' *Studies in Higher Education*, 30(3): 257–74.

Kogan, M. (1986) *Education Accountability: an analytic overview*, London: Hutchinson.

Kruger, M.L., van Eck, E. and Vermeulen, A. (2005) 'Why principals leave: risk factors for premature departure in the Netherlands compared for women and men', *School Leadership and Management*, 25(3): 241–61.

Laing, C. and Robinson, A. (2003) 'The withdrawal of non-traditional students: developing an explanatory model', *Journal of Further and Higher Education*, 27(2): 175–85.

Lakomski, G. (2001) 'Organisational change, leadership and learning: culture as a cognitive process', *The International Journal of Educational Management*, 15(2): 68–77.

Lam, S., Yim, P. and Lam, T. (2002) 'Transforming school culture: can collaboration be initiated?' *Educational Research*, 44(2): 181–204.

Lambert, L. (2003) 'Leadership redefined: an evocative context for teacher leadership', *School Leadership and Management*, 23(4): 421–30.

Lauder, H. and Hughes, D. (1999) *Trading in Futures: why markets in education don't work*, Buckingham: Open University Press.

Law, S. (1999) 'Leadership for learning: the changing culture of professional development in schools', *Journal of Educational Administration*, 37(1): 66–79.

Law, S. and Glover, D. (1996) *Towards Coherence in the Management of Professional Development Planning*, Cambridge: BEMAS Research Conference.

—— (2000) *Educational Leadership and Learning: practice, policy and research*, Buckingham: Open University Press.

Learmouth, J. (2000) *Inspection: what's in it for schools*, London: RoutledgeFalmer.

Leithwood, K. (1994) 'The move towards transformational leadership', *Educational Leadership*, 49(5): 8–12.

—— (1999) *Educational Accountability: the state of the art*, Gutersloh: Bertelsmann Foundation Publishers.

—— (2001) 'School leadership in the context of accountability policies', *International Journal of Leadership in Education*, 4(3): 217–35.

Leithwood, K. and Jantzi, D. (2000) 'The effects of different sources of leadership on student engagement in school', in K. Riley and K.S. Louis (eds) *Leadership for Change and School Reform: international perspectives*, New York: RoutledgeFalmer.

Leithwood, K. and Montgomery, D. (1982) 'The role of the elementary principal in program improvement', *Review of Educational Research*, 52(3): 309–39.

Leithwood, K.A. and Riehl, C. (2003) *What Do We Know About Successful School Leadership?* Philadelphia, PA: Laboratory for Student Success, Temple University.

Leithwood, K., Day, C., Sammons, P., Harris, A. and Hopkins, D. (2006) *Seven Strong Claims about Successful School Leadership*, Nottingham: National College for School Leadership.

Leung, C. (2005) 'Accountability versus school development: self-evaluation in an international school in Hong Kong', *International Studies in Educational Administration*, 33(1): 2–14.

Levačić, R. (1997) 'Managing resources in educational institutions: an open systems approach', in M. Preedy, R. Glatter and R. Levačić (eds) *Educational Management: strategy, quality and resources*, Buckingham: Open University Press.

—— (2002) 'Efficiency, equity and autonomy', in T. Bush and L. Bell (eds) *The Principles and Practice of Educational Management*, London: Paul Chapman Publishing.

Levačić, R. and Vignoles, A. (2002) 'Researching the links between school resources and student outcomes in the UK: a review of issues and evidence', *Education Economics*, 10(3): 312–31.

Lewis, R. and Burman, E. (2008) 'Providing for student voice in classroom management: teachers' views', *International Journal of Inclusive Education*, 12(2): 151–67.

Lieberman, J. (2009) 'Reinventing teacher professional norms and identities: the role of lesson study and learning communities', *Professional Development in Education*, 35(1): 83–99.

Liston, C. (1999) *Managing Quality and Standards*, Buckingham: Open University Press.

Literacy Task Force (1997) *The Implementation of the National Literacy Strategy*, London: DfEE.

Little, B. (2005) 'Policies towards work-focused higher education – are they meeting employers' needs?' *Tertiary Education and Management*, 11(2): 131–46.

Livingston, K. and McCall, J. (2005) 'Evaluation: judgemental or developmental?' *European Journal of Teacher Education*, 28(2): 165–78.

Logan, E. and Feiler, A. (2006) 'Forging links between parents and schools: a new role for teaching assistants?' *Support for Learning*, 21(3): 115–20.

LSC (Learning and Skills Council) (2006) *Framework for Excellence*. Online. Available http://www.ffe.gov.uk (accessed September 2009).

LSN (Learning and Skills Network) (2009) *About LSN*. Online. Available http://www.lsneducation.org.uk/about/ (accessed January 2009).

Lumby, J. (2001) *Managing Further Education Colleges: learning enterprise*, London: Paul Chapman Publishing.

—— (2002) 'The management of sixth form colleges: implications for leadership', paper presented at the Annual Conference of the British Educational Research Association, University of Exeter, 12–14 September 2002. Online. Available http://www.leeds.ac.uk/educol/documents/00002438.htm (accessed January 2010).

Lumby, J. and Foskett, N. (1999) (eds) *Managing External Relations in Schools and Colleges*, London: Paul Chapman Publishing.

Lumby, J. and Wilson, M. (2003) 'Developing 14–19 education: meeting needs and improving choice', *Journal of Education Policy*, 18(5): 533–50.

Lyotard, J.F. (1984) *The Post-modern Condition: a report on knowledge*, Minneapolis: University of Minnesota Press and Manchester: University of Manchester Press.

MacBeath, J. (1999) *Schools Must Speak for Themselves: arguments for school self-evaluation (what's in it for schools)*, London: Routledge.

—— (2005) 'Leadership as distributed: a matter of practice', *School Leadership and Management*, 25(4): 349–66.

—— (2006) 'The talent enigma', *International Journal of Leadership in Education*, 9(3): 183–204.

MacBeath, J. and Dempster, N. (2009) (eds) *Connecting Leadership and Learning: principles for practice*, London: Routledge.

MacBeath, J. and MacBeath, M. (2002) *The Self-Evaluation File: good ideas and practical tools for teachers, pupils and school leaders*, Edinburgh: Learning Files Scotland Ltd.

MacBeath, J. and McGlynn, A. (2002) *Self-Evaluation: what's in it for schools?* London: Routledge.

MacBeath, J., Schratz, M., Meuret, D. and Jakobsen, L. (2000) *Self-Evaluation in European Schools: a story of change*, London: RoutledgeFalmer.

MacBeath, J., Gray, J., Cullen, J., Frost, D., Steward, S. and Swaffield, S. (2007) *Schools on the Edge: responding to challenging circumstances*, London: Paul Chapman Publishing.

McCall, M.W. (1998) *High Flyers: developing the next generation of leaders*, Boston, MA: Harvard Business School Press.

McCrystal, P. and McAleer, J. (2003) 'Managing NVQs in the further and higher education sector ten years after their introduction', *Journal of Further and Higher Education*, 27(3): 289–305.

McCulloch, G., Helsby, G. and Knight, P. (2000) *The Politics of Professionalism, Teachers and the Curriculum*, London: Continuum.

McDonald, B. and Boud, D. (2003) 'The impact of self-assessment on achievement: the effects of self-assessment training on performance in external examinations', *Assessment in Education*, 10(2): 209–20.

MacGilchrist, B. (2000) 'Improving self-improvement?' *Research Papers in Education*, 15(3): 325–38.

McLaughlin, T. (2005) 'The educative importance of ethos', *British Journal of Educational Studies*, 53(3): 306–25.

Maclure, S. (2001) *The Inspectors' Calling: HMI and the shaping of educational policy 1945–1992*, London: Hodder and Stoughton.

McMahon, A. (2001) 'A cultural perspective on school effectiveness, school improvement and teacher professional development', in A. Harris and N. Bennett (eds) *School Effectiveness and School Improvement: alternative perspectives*, London: Continuum.

McMahon, A., Bolam, R., Abbott, R. and Holly, P. (1984) *Guidelines for Review and Internal Development in Schools: primary and secondary school handbooks*, Harlow: Longman.

McNamara, G. and O'Hara, J. (2005) 'Internal review and self-evaluation – the chosen route to school improvement in Ireland?' *Studies in Educational Evaluation*, 31(4): 267–82.

—— (2006) 'Workable compromise or pointless exercise? School-based evaluation in the Irish context', *Educational Management Administration and Leadership*, 34(4): 567–86.

—— (2008) 'The importance of the concept of self-evaluation in the changing landscape of education policy', *Studies in Educational Evaluation*, 34(3): 173–79.

McNay, I (1995) 'From the collegial academy to the corporate enterprise: the changing culture of universities', in T. Shuller (ed.) *The Changing University?* Buckingham: Society for Research in Higher Education and Open University Press.

MacNeil, A., Prater, D. and Busch, S. (2009) 'The effects of school culture and climate on student achievement', *International Journal of Leadership in Education*, 12(1): 73–84.

McWilliam, E. and Perry, L. (2006) 'On being more accountable: the push and pull of risk in school leadership', *International Journal of Leadership in Education*, 9(2): 97–109.

Marks, A. (2000) 'In search of the "local" university: considering issues of access for mature learners', *Journal of Further and Higher Education*, 24(3): 363–71.

Marsh, J. (1992) *The Quality Toolkit*, London: IFS.

Marshall, J.D. (2004) 'Performativity: Lyotard and Foucault through Searle and Austin', *Studies in Philosophy and Education*, 18(5): 309–17.

Martin, N., Worrall, N. and Dutson-Steinfeld, A. (2005) 'Student voice: Pandora's box or philosopher's stone?', paper presented at the International Congress for School Effectiveness and School Improvement, Barcelona, Spain, 2–5 January 2005.

Martinez, P. (1999) *Learning from Continuous Professional Development*, London: Further Education Development Agency.

—— (2002) 'Effectiveness and improvement: school and college research compared', *Research in Post-Compulsory Education*, 7(1): 97–118.

Merchant, G. and Marsh, J. (1998) *Co-ordinating Primary Language and Literacy, the Subject Leader's Handbook*, London: Paul Chapman Publishing.

Middlehurst, R. (1992) 'Quality: an organising principle for higher education?', *Higher Education Quarterly*, 46(1): 75–92.

Milbourne, L., Macrae, S. and Maguire, M. (2003) 'Collaborative solutions or new policy problems: exploring multi-agency partnerships in education and health work', *Journal of Education Policy*, 18(1): 19–35.

Mistry, M., Burton, N. and Brundrett, M. (2004) 'Managing LSAs: an evaluation of the use of learning support assistants in an urban primary school', *School Leadership and Management*, 24(2): 125–37.

Mitra, D. (2005) 'Increasing student voice and moving towards youth leadership', *The Prevention Researcher*, 13(1): 7–10.

Mitra, D.L. (2008) *Student Voice in School Reform*, New York: State University of New York Press.

Mitsoni, F. (2006) '"I get bored when we don't have the opportunity to say our opinion": learning about teaching from students', *Educational Review*, 58(2): 159–70.

Moos, L. (2005) 'How do schools bridge the gap between external demands for accountability and the need for internal trust?' *Journal of Educational Change*, 6(4): 307–28.

Morley, A. (2006) 'The development of leadership capacity in a school facing challenging circumstances', in M. Ainscow and M. West (eds) *Improving Urban Schools: leadership and collaboration*, Maidenhead: Open University Press.

Morley, L. (2003) *Quality and Power in Higher Education*, Buckingham: Open University Press.

—— (2005) 'Opportunity or exploitation? Women and quality assurance in higher education', *Gender and Education*, 17(4): 411–29.

Mortimore, P. and Whitty, G. (1997) *Can School Improvement Overcome the Effects of Disadvantage?* London: Institute of Education, University of London.

Muijs, D. and Harris, A. (2003) 'Teacher leadership – improvement through empowerment? An overview of the literature', *Educational Management and Administration*, 31(4): 437–48.

Muijs, D., Harris, A., Chapman, C., Stoll, L. and Russ, J. (2004) 'Improving schools in socioeconomically disadvantaged areas – a review of research evidence', *School Effectiveness and School Improvement*, 15(2): 149–75.

Muijs, D., Harris, A., Lumby, J., Morrison, M. and Sood, K. (2006) 'Leadership and leadership development in highly effective further education providers. Is there a relationship?' *Journal of Further and Higher Education*, 30(1): 87–106.

Mukhopadhyay, M. (2005) *Total Quality Management in Education*, London: Sage.

Munro-Faure, L. and Munro-Faure, M. (1992) *Implementing Total Quality*, London: Pitman.

Murgatroyd, S. and Morgan, C. (1993) *Total Quality Management and the School*, Milton Keynes: Open University Press.

NAHT (National Association of Head Teachers) (2007) *The Quick Reference Handbook for School Leaders*, London: Paul Chapman Publishing.

Nauffal, D.I. (2004) 'Higher education in Lebanon: management cultures and their impact on performance outcomes', unpublished PhD thesis, School of Education, University of Birmingham, UK.

NCSL (National College for School Leadership) (2006a) *Leadership Succession: an overview*. Online. Available http://www.nationalcollege.org.uk/docinfo?id = 17247&filename = leadership-succession-overview.pdf (accessed 5 December 2006).

—— (2006b) *Succession Planning: formal advice to the Secretary of State*. Online. Available http://www.nationalcollege.org.uk/succession-planning-national-college-advice-2.pdf (accessed 5 December 2006).

—— (2007) *Recruiting Headteachers and Senior Leaders: overview of research findings*. Online. Available http://www.ncsl.org.uk/publications (accessed 12 April 2007).

Neil, P. and Johnston, J. (2003) 'An approach to analysing professional discourse in a school self-evaluation project', *Research in Education*, 73(1): 73–86.

Neil, P., McEwen, A., Carlisle, K. and Knipe, D. (2001) 'The self-evaluating school: a case study of a special school', *British Journal of Special Education*, 28(4): 174–81.

Nevo, D. (2001) 'School evaluation: internal or external?' *Studies in Educational Evaluation*, 27(2): 95–106.

Newman, S. and Jahdi, K. (2009) 'Marketisation of education: marketing, rhetoric and reality', *Journal of Further and Higher Education*, 33(1): 1–11.

Nightingale, P. and O'Neil, M. (1994) *Achieving Quality Learning in Higher Education*, London: Kogan Page.

Nolan Committee (1997) *Standards of Conduct in Local Government*, London: HMSO.

Ofsted (1995) *Guidance on Inspection*, London: Ofsted.

—— (2003a) *Ofsted Handbook*, London: Ofsted.

—— (2003b) *Taking the First Step Forward . . . towards an Education for Sustainable Development*, Annex C, London: Ofsted.

—— (2005) *Ofsted Handbook*, London: Ofsted.

—— (2007) *Raising Standards, Improving Lives*, London: The Office for Standards in Education.

—— (2008a) *What We Do*. Online. Available http://www.ofsted.gov.uk/portal/site/Internet/menuitem.455968b0530071c4828a0d8308c08a0c/?vgnextoid = e99c8587fd24a010VgnVCM 1000008192a8c0RCRD (accessed November 2008).

—— (2008b) *A Focus on Improvement*, London: Ofsted.

—— (2008c) *The Annual Report of Her Majesty's Chief Inspector of Education, Children's Services and Skills 2007/08*, London: The Stationery Office.

Oldroyd, D. (2005) 'Human Resources for Learning', in M. Coleman and P. Earley, *Leadership and Management in Education: cultures, change and context*, Oxford: Oxford University Press.

Oplatka, I. and Hemsley-Brown, J. (2004) 'The research on school marketing: current issues and future directions', *Journal of Educational Administration*, 42(3): 375–400.

Osler, A., Watling R. and Busher, H. (2000) *Reasons for Exclusion from School: report to the DfEE*, Leicester: Centre for Citizenship, School of Education, University of Leicester.

Ozga, J. and Sukhnandan, L. (1998) 'Undergraduate non-completion: developing an explanatory model', *Higher Education Quarterly*, 52(3): 316–33.

Ozolins, L., Hall, H. and Peterson, R. (2008) 'The student voice: recognising the hidden and informal curriculum in medicine', *Medical Teacher*, 30(6): 606–11.

Paletta, A. and Vidoni, D. (2006) 'Italian school managers: a complex identity', *International Studies in Educational Administration*, 34(1): 46–70.

Palmer, J. (2001) 'Student drop-out: a case-study in new managerialist policy', *Journal of Further and Higher Education*, 25(3): 349–57.

Papatheodorou, T. (2002) 'How we like our school to be . . . pupil's voices', *European Educational Research Journal*, 1(3): 445–67.

Pennsylvania Department of Education (2007) *A Framework for Continuous School Improvement Planning*, Pittsburgh, PA: Pennsylvania Department of Education.

Person, A.E. and Rosenbaum, J.E. (2006) 'Educational outcomes of labor-market linking and job placement for students at public and private 2-year colleges', *Economics of Education Review*, 25(4): 412–29.

Peters, J. (2002) 'Expecting too much from school/university partnerships for school improvement', paper presented at the Annual Conference of the British Educational Research Association, University of Exeter, 12–14 September. Online. Available http://www.leeds.ac.uk/educol/documents/00002132.htm (accessed September 2008).

Peters, T. (1989) *Thriving on Chaos*, London: Pan.

—— (1992) *Thriving on Chaos,* New York: Knopf.

Peters, T. and Waterman, R.H. (1982) *In Search of Excellence: lessons from America's best-run companies*, New York: Profile Business.

Peterson, S., Kovel-Jarboe, P. and Schwartz, S. (1997) 'Quality improvement in higher education: implications for student retention', *Quality in Higher Education*, 3(2): 131–41.

Pinkus, S. (2006) 'Applying a family systems perspective for understanding parent-professional relationships: a study of families located in the Anglo-Jewish community', *Support for Learning*, 21(3): 156–61.

Pollard, A. and James, M. (2004) *Personalised Learning: a commentary by the Teaching and Learning Research Programme*, London: TLRP/ESRC.

Poore, P. (2005) 'School culture: the space between the bars; the silence between the notes', *Journal of Research in International Education*, 4(3): 351–61.

Pounder, J.S. (2006) 'Transformational classroom leadership: the fourth wave of teacher leadership?' *Educational Management Administration and Leadership*, 34(4): 535–47.

Preedy, M., Glatter, R. and Levačić, R. (1997) (eds) *Educational Management: strategy, quality and resources*, Buckingham: Open University Press.

PricewaterhouseCoopers (2007) *Independent Study into School Leadership RB818,* Nottingham: DfES Publications.

Prichard, C. (2000) *Making Managers in Universities and Colleges*, Buckingham: Open University Press.

Prosser, J. (1999) *School Culture*, London: Paul Chapman Publishing.

Purkey, S. and Smith, M. (1983) 'Effective schools: a review', *Elementary School Journal*, 83(4): 426–52.

QAA (Quality Assurance Agency) (2000) *Effective Learning and Teaching in Higher Education*, London: QAA.

QIA (Quality Improvement Agency for Lifelong Learning) (2009a) *About the Quality Assurance Agency for Higher Education*. Online. Available http://www.qaa.ac.uk/aboutus/default.asp (accessed January 2009).

—— (2009b) *Background to the QIA*. Online. Available http://www.qia.org.uk (accessed Janaury 2009).

Rand, M.K. and Shelton-Colangelo, S. (2002) *Voices of Student Teachers: cases from the field*, New York: Allyn and Bacon.

Reeves, J. and Forde, C. (2004) 'The social dynamics of changing practice', *Cambridge Journal of Education*, 34(1): 85–102.

Reezigt, G. and Creemers, B. (2005) 'A comprehensive framework for effective school improvement', *School Effectiveness and School Improvement*, 16(4): 407–24.

Rhodes, C. and Brundrett, M. (2010) 'Leadership for learning', in T. Bush and L. Bell (eds) *The Principles and Practice of Educational Leadership and Management* (2nd edn), London: Sage.

Rhodes, C. and Nevill, A. (2004) 'Academic and social integration in higher education: a survey of satisfaction and dissatisfaction within a first-year education studies cohort at a new university', *Journal of Further and Higher Education*, 28(2): 179–93.

Rhodes, C.P. (2001) *Resource Management for Schools: a handbook for staff development activities*, London: David Fulton Publishers.

—— (2006) 'The impact of leadership and management on the construction of the professional identity in school learning mentors', *Educational Studies*, 32(2): 157–69.

Rhodes, C.P. and Beneicke, S. (2002) 'Coaching, mentoring and peer-networking: challenges for the management of teacher professional development in schools', *Journal of In-Service Education*, 28(2): 297–309.

—— (2003) 'Professional development support for poorly performing teachers: challenges and opportunities for school managers in addressing teacher learning needs', *Journal of In-Service Education*, 29(1): 123–40.

Rhodes, C.P. and Brundrett, M. (2006) 'The identification, development, succession and retention of leadership talent in contextually different primary schools: a case study located within the English West Midlands', *School Leadership and Management*, 26(3): 269–87.

—— (2008) 'What makes my school a good training ground for leadership development?' *Management in Education*, 22(1): 21–27.

—— (2009) 'Growing the leadership talent pool: perceptions of heads, middle leaders and classroom teachers about professional development and leadership succession planning within their own schools', *Professional Development in Education*, 35(3),381–98.

Rhodes, C.P. and Houghton-Hill, S. (2000) 'The linkage of continuing professional development and the classroom experience of pupils: barriers perceived by senior managers in some secondary schools', *Journal of In-Service Education*, 26(3): 423–35.

Rhodes, C.P., Bateman, J. and Farr, J. (2005) 'Partnership or parallelism? Modelling university support for teacher research in schools', *Professional Development Today*, Summer 2005, 25–30.

Rhodes, C.P., Bill, K., Biscomb, K., Nevill, A. and Bruneau, S. (2002) 'Widening participation in higher education: support at the further education/higher education interface and its impact on the transition and progression of advanced GNVQ students', *Journal of Vocational Education and Training*, 54(1): 133–45.

Rhodes, C.P., Brundrett, M. and Nevill, A. (2008) 'Leadership talent identification and development', *Educational Management Administration and Leadership*, 36(3): 311–35.

Rhodes, C.P., Nevill, A. and Allan, J. (2004a) 'Valuing and supporting teachers: a survey of teacher satisfaction, dissatisfaction, morale and retention in an English local education authority', *Research in Education*, 71(1): 67–80.

Rhodes, C.P., Stokes, M. and Hampton, G. (2004b) *A Practical Guide to Mentoring, Coaching and Peer-Networking: teacher professional development in schools and colleges*, London: RoutledgeFalmer.

Roberts, S. and Pruitt, E. (2003) *Schools as Professional Learning Communities*, London: Sage.

Robinson, C. and Sebba, J. (2005) *A Review of Research and Evaluation to Inform the Development of a New Postgraduate Professional Development Programme*. Online. Available http://www.tda.gov.uk (accessed September 2009).

Rogers, G. and Badham, L. (1992) *Evaluation in Schools*, London: Routledge.

Romzek, B.S. (2000) 'Dynamics of public accountability in an era of reform', *International Review of Administrative Sciences*, 66(1): 21–44.

Rosenholtz, S. (1989) *Teachers' Workplace: the social organisation of schools*, New York: Longman.

Rothwell, W.J. (2005) *Effective Succession Planning: ensuring leadership continuity and building talent from within* (3rd edn), New York: American Management Association.

Rowe, K.J. and Sykes, J. (1989) 'The impact of professional development on teachers' self-perceptions', *Teaching and Teacher Education*, 5(2): 129–41.

Rudd, P. and Davis, D. (2000) 'Evaluating school self-evaluation', paper presented at the Annual Conference of the British Educational Research Association, Cardiff University, 7–9 September.

Rudduck, J. and Flutter, J. (2000) 'Pupil participation and perspective: "carving a new order of experience"', *Cambridge Journal of Education*, 30(1): 75–89.

—— (2003) *How to Improve Your School*, London: Continuum.

Rudduck, J. and McIntyre, D. (2007) *Improving Learning Through Consulting Pupils*, London: Routledge.

Rustemier, S. (1999) 'Cultures of inclusion in further education', paper presented at the Annual Conference of the British Educational Research Association, University of Sussex, 1–5 September.

Rutherford, D. (2005) 'The impact of leadership in primary schools', *Management in Education*, 18(5): 21–26.

Ryan, J.F. (2005) 'Institutional expenditures and student engagement: a role for financial resources in enhancing student learning and development?' *Research in Higher Education*, 46(2): 235–49.

Ryan, K.E. (2004) 'Serving the public interests in educational accountability', *American Journal of Evaluation*, 25(4): 443–60.

—— (2005) 'Making educational accountability more democratic', *American Journal of Evaluation*, 26(4): 532–43.

Sallis, E. (2002) *Total Quality Management in Education* (3rd edn), London: Kogan Page.

Sanders, M.G. and Lewis, K.C. (2005) 'Building bridges toward excellence: community involvement in high schools', *The High School Journal*, February/March 2005, 1–9.

Sarason, S. (1982) *The Culture of the School and the Problem of Change*, Massachusetts: Allyn and Bacon.

Saunders, M. and Machell, J. (2000) 'Understanding emerging trends in higher education curricula and work connections', *Higher Education Policy*, 13(3): 287–302.

Schein, E.H. (1997) *Organizational Culture and Leadership*, San Francisco, CA: Jossey Bass.

Scott, D. (1999) 'Accountability in education systems', in J. Lumby and N. Foskett (eds) *Managing External Relations in Schools and Colleges*, London: Paul Chapman Publishing.

Senge, P.M., Kleiner, A., Roberts, C., Ross, R.B., and Smith, B.J. (1996) *The Fifth Discipline Fieldbook*, London: Nicholas Brealey.

Sergiovanni, T.J. (1992) *Moral Leadership: getting to the heart of school improvement*, San Francisco, CA: Jossey-Bass.

—— (2001) *Leadership: what's in it for schools?* London: RoutledgeFalmer.

Shah, S. (2004) 'The researcher/interviewer in intercultural context: a social intruder', *British Educational Research Journal*, 30(4): 549–75.

—— (2006) 'Educational leadership: an Islamic perspective', *British Educational Research Journal*, 32(3): 363–85.

Shann, M. (1999) 'Academics and a culture of caring: the relationship between school achievement and prosocial and antisocial behaviors in four urban middle schools', *School Effectiveness and School Improvement*, 10(4): 390–413.

Shayer, M. and Adey, P. (2002) *Learning Intelligence*, Buckingham: Open University Press.

Sheppard, B. (1996) 'Exploring the transformational nature of instructional leadership', *Alberta Journal of Educational Research*, 42(4): 325–44.

Shortland, S. (2004) 'Peer observation: a tool for staff development or compliance?' *Journal of Further and Higher Education*, 28(2): 219–28.

Silcock, P. (2002) 'Can we manage teacher performance?' *Education 3–13*, 30(3): 23–27.

Silcock, P. and Brundrett, M. (2002) *Competence, Success and Excellence in Teaching*, London: RoutledgeFalmer.

—— (2006) 'Pedagogy at Key Stage 2: teaching through pupil-teacher partnership', in R. Webb (ed.) *Changing Teaching and Learning in the Primary School*, Maidenhead: Open University Press.

Silins, H. and Mulford, B. (2002) 'Leadership and school results', in K. Leithwood, P. Hallinger,

K.S. Louis, P. Furman-Brown, P. Gronn, W. Mulford and K. Riley (eds) *Second International Handbook of Educational Leadership and Administration*, Netherlands: Kluwer.

Simkins, T. and Lumby, J. (2002) 'Cultural transformation in further education? Mapping the debate', *Research in Post-Compulsory Education*, 7(1): 9–25.

Smith, R.E. (2002) 'The role of the university head of department: a survey in two British universities', *Educational Management and Administration*, 30(3): 293–312.

—— (2005) 'Departmental leadership and management in chartered and statutory universities: a case of diversity', *Educational Management Administration and Leadership*, 33(4): 449–64.

Solvason, C. (2005) 'Investigating specialist school ethos . . . or do you mean culture?' *Educational Studies*, 31(1): 85–94.

Southworth, G. (2000) 'How primary schools learn', *Research Papers in Education*, 15(3), 275–91.

—— (2004) *Primary School Leadership in Context: leading small, medium and large schools*, London: RoutledgeFalmer.

Sparkes, A. (1991) 'The culture of teaching, critical reflection and change', *Educational Management and Administration*, 19(1): 4–18.

Spillane, J. (2004) 'Educational leadership', *Educational Evaluation and Policy Analysis*, 26(2): 169–72.

Staessens, K. and Vandenberghe, R. (1994) 'Vision as a core component in school culture', *Journal of Curriculum Studies*, 26(2): 187–200.

Steingard, D.S. and Fitzgibbons, D.E. (1993) 'A postmodern deconstruction of total quality management', *Journal of Organizational Change Management*, 6(5): 27–42.

Stenhouse, L. (1975) *An Introduction to Curriculum Research and Development*, London: Heinemann.

Stewart, J. and Walsh, K. (1990) *In Search of Quality*, Luton: Local Government Management Board.

Stoll, L. and Fink, D. (1996) *Changing Our Schools*, Milton Keynes: Open University Press.

Stoll, L. and Louis, K.S. (2007) *Professional Learning Communities: divergence, depths and dilemmas*, Maidenhead: Open University Press.

Stoll, L. and Temperley, J. (2009) 'Creative leadership teams: capacity building and succession planning', *Management in Education*, 23(1): 12–18.

Stoll, L., Fink, D. and Earl, L. (2003) *It's All About Learning and It's About Time*, Buckingham: Open University Press.

Stoll, L., Bolam, R., McMahon, A., Thomas, S., Wallace, M., Greenwood, A. and Hawkey, K. (2006) *What is a Professional Learning Community? A summary*, DfES-0187–2006, London: DfES.

Strydom, J.F., Zulu, N. and Murray, L. (2004) 'Quality, culture and change', *Quality in Higher Education*, 10(3): 207–17.

Sugrue, C. (2002) 'Irish teachers' experiences of professional learning: implications for policy and practice', *Journal of In-Service Education*, 28(2): 311–38.

Sutton, M (1997) 'Allocating budgets for curriculum support', in M. Preedy, R. Glatter and R. Levačić (eds) *Educational Management: strategy, quality and resources*, Buckingham: Open University Press.

Swaffield, S. (2003) 'Self evaluation and the role of a critical friend', *Managing Schools Today*, 12(5): 28–30.

—— (2004) 'Critical friends: supporting leadership, improving learning', *Improving Schools*, 7(3): 267–78.

Swaffield, S. and MacBeath, J. (2005) 'School self-evaluation and the role of a critical friend', *Cambridge Journal of Education*, 35(2): 239–52.

—— (2009) 'Leadership for learning', in J. MacBeath and N. Dempster (eds) *Connecting Leadership and Learning: principles for practice*, London: Routledge.

Szanto, T.R. (2005) 'Evaluations of the third kind: external evaluations of external quality assurance agencies', *Quality in Higher Education*, 11(3): 183–93.

TDA (Training and Development Agency for Schools) (2006a) *Targeted Youth Support Toolkit, Process Guide – Stakeholder Mapping*, London: Training and Development Agency for Schools.

—— (2006b) *The Core Offer*. Online. Available http://www.tda.gov.uk/Home/remodelling/extendedschools/coreoffer.aspx (accessed October 2009).

Temple, P. (2006) 'Intervention in a higher education market: a case study', *Higher Education Quarterly*, 60(3): 257–69.

Tett, L., Crowther, J. and O'Hara, P. (2003) 'Collaborative partnerships in community education', *Journal of Education Policy*, 18(1): 37–51.

The American Society for Quality (2008) *Quality in Education*. Online. Available http://www.asq.org/education/why-quality/common-issues.html (accessed January 2008).

Thomas, G. (1997) 'School inspection and school improvement', paper presented to the Annual Conference of the British Educational Research Association, University of York 10–14 September.

Thomas, H. and Martin, J. (1996) *Managing Resources for School Improvement: creating a cost-effective school*, London: Routledge.

Thornton, M., Bricheno, P. and Reid, I. (2002) 'Students' reasons for wanting to teach in primary school', *Research in Education*, 67: 33–43.

Tigelaar, D., Dolmans, D., Wolfhagen, I. and van der Vleuten, C. (2004) 'The development and validation of a framework for teaching competencies in higher education', *Higher Education*, 48(2): 253–68.

Tondeur, J., Devos, G., Van Houtte, M., Van Braak, J. and Valcke, M. (2009) 'Understanding structural and cultural school characteristics in relation to educational change: the case of ICT integration', *Educational Studies*, 35(2): 223–35.

TSO (2004) *Every Child Matters: change for children*, London: TSO.

—— (2007) *The Children's Plan: building brighter futures*, London: TSO.

TTA (Teacher Training Agency) (1998) *National Standards for Subject Leaders,* London: Teacher Training Agency.

US Congress (2002) *No Child Left Behind*, Washington: US Congress.

Van der Westhuizen, L.J. and Fourie, M. (2002) 'Quality assurance in international, African and Southern African contexts', in H. Griesel, A.H. Strydom and L.J. Van der Westhuizen (eds) *Quality Assurance in a Transforming University System: lessons and challenges*, Bloemfontain: CLF.

Van Voorhis and Sheldon, S. (2004) 'Principals' roles in the development of US programs of school, family, and community partnerships', *International Journal of Educational Research*, 41(1): 55–70.

Visscher, A. and Witziers, B. (2004) 'Subject departments as professional communities?' *British Educational Research Journal*, 30(6): 785–800.

Wallace, M. (2002) 'Modelling distributed leadership and management effectiveness: primary senior management teams in England and Wales', *School Effectiveness and School Improvement*, 13(2): 163–86.

Walsh, K. (1994) 'Quality surveillance and performance measurement', in K.A. Riley and D.L. Nutall, *Measuring Quality Education Indicators – United Kingdom and International Perspectives*, London: Falmer Press.

Walsh, P. (2006) 'Narrowed horizons and the impoverishment of educational discourse: teaching, learning and performing under the new educational bureaucracies', *Journal of Education Policy*, 21(1): 95–117.

Waring, S. (1999) 'Finding your way: sensing the external environment', in J. Lumby and

N. Foskett (eds) *Managing External Relations in Schools and Colleges*, London: Paul Chapman Publishing.

Warwick, P. and Cunningham, P. (2006) 'Progressive alternatives? Teachers' experience of autonomy and accountability in the school community', *Education 3–13*, 34(1): 27–36.

Watt, S. and Paterson, L.C. (2000) 'Pathways and partnerships: widening access to higher education', *Journal of Further and Higher Education*, 24(1): 107–16.

Webb, R. (2005) 'Leading teaching and learning in the primary school: from educative leadership to pedagogical leadership', *Educational Management Administration and Leadership*, 33(1): 69–91.

Webb, R., Vulliamy, G., Hakkinen, K. and Hamalainen, S. (1998) 'External inspection or school self-evaluation? A comparative analysis of policy and practice in primary schools in England and Finland', *British Educational Research Journal*, 24(5): 539–57.

Webb, T.P. (2005) 'The anatomy of accountability', *Journal of Education Policy*, 20(2): 189–208.

Weller, D. L. (1998) 'Unlocking the culture for quality schools: reengineering', *International Journal of Educational Management*, 12(6), 250–59.

West-Burnham, J. (1992) *Managing Quality in Schools: a TQM approach*, Harlow: Longman.

—— (1994) 'Inspection, evaluation and quality assurance', in T. Bush and J. West-Burnham, *The Principles of Educational Management*, Harlow: Longman.

—— (1995) *Total Quality Management in Education*, University of Leicester: EMDU.

Whitty, G. and Wisby, E. (2007) 'Whose voice? An exploration of the current policy interest in school decision-making', *International Studies in Sociology of Education*, 17(3): 303–19.

Wolfe, R. (1996) *Systematic Succession Planning: building leadership from within*, Menlo Park, CA: Crisp Publications Inc.

Wragg, E.C., Haynes, G.S., Wragg, C.M. and Chamberlin, R.P. (2000) *Failing Teachers?* London: Routledge.

Wroe, A. and Halsall, R. (1999) 'School self-evaluation: measurement and reflection in the school improvement process', *Research in Education*, 65: 41–52.

Yorke, M. (1995) 'Self-scrutiny of quality in higher education: a questionnaire', *Quality Assurance in Education*, 3(1): 10–13.

—— (2000) 'The quality of student experience: what can institutions learn from data relating to non-completion?' *Quality in Higher Education*, 6(1): 61–75.

Zaccaro, S.J. (2007) 'Trait-based perspectives of leadership', *American Psychologist*, 62(1): 6–16.

Zaccaro, S.J., Kemp, C. and Bader, P. (2004) 'Leaders' traits and attributes', in J. Antonakis, A.T. Cianciolo and R.J. Sternberg (eds) *The Nature of Leadership*, Thousand Oaks, CA: Sage.

Index